CROSS COUNTRY SKI INNS

CROSS COUNTRY

SKI INNS
OF THE EASTERN U.S. AND CANADA

text by Marge Lamy

with photographs by George W. Gardner

designed and produced by Robert R. Reid

THE STEPHEN GREENE PRESS

Lexington, Massachusetts

Photograph on page 1 taken at Mountain Top Ski Resort, Vermont.
Photographs on pages 2 and 3 taken at Far Hills Inn, Quebec, Canada.

Text copyright © Robert Reid Associates, 1986
Photographs copyright © George W. Gardner, 1986

First published in 1986 by The Stephen Greene Press, Inc.
Published simultaneously in Canada by Penguin Books of Canada Limited.
Distributed by Viking Penguin Inc., 40 West 23rd Street, New York, NY 10010.

The photographs on pages 83 and 87 used by permission of William T. Sievert.
The photograph on page 84 used by permission of Peter Lemon.
All other photographs are by George W. Gardner.

Library of Congress Cataloging-in-Publication Data

Lamy, Marge.
   Cross country ski inns of the eastern U.S. & Canada.

  1. Ski resorts—Northeastern states—Directories.
2. Ski resorts—Canada—Directories. 3. Cross-country
skiing—Northeastern States. 4. Cross-country
skiing—Canada. 5. Hotels, taverns, etc.—
Northeastern States—Directories. 6. Hotels, taverns,
etc.—Canada—Directories. I. Gardner, George William,
1940–   . II. Title.
GV854.35.U6L36 1986   796.93′025′7   96-12069
ISBN 0-8289-0569-X 5

A Robert Reid Associates production.
Printed and bound in Hong Kong by South Sea International Press, Ltd.
Typeset in Trump Mediaeval and Spartan Light by the Monotype Composition Company, Baltimore.

CONTENTS

FOREWORD

Where variety is the spice of life

THE AFFINITY between country inns and cross country skiing is extraordinary. Both attract people who enjoy the outdoors and "doing it on your own." Cross country skiers aren't pressured to dress stylishly or use expensive equipment. Nor do they feel it is necessary to ski particularly well to have fun. For most, aside from the health benefits, it's primarily a way to cheat the winter doldrums.

This laid-back approach matches the philosophy of those who choose the inn business. Because of the atmosphere innkeepers create, more people are finding that staying at an inn is thoroughly relaxing. It's a pleasure to step out of today's madcap pace and acquaint ourselves with our common heritage. Most innkeepers have an acute sense of what made living good in the past. They recreate it through the loving restoration of old homes, inns or hotels and the retrieval of furnishings from an era when individual craftsmanship was prized.

To that, they add the best of the modern: fine food, wine or spirits, and good company. It isn't unusual for guests to return year after year at the same time to meet friends made at an inn. This holds true regardless of the size of the establishment.

The strength of this book lies in the diversity of choices for potential travelers. There are modest inns and plush ones, places where ski clothes are the accepted garb and others where one can or should dress for dinner. Every inn has access to good skiing, usually beginning at the door and always within close range.

A couple of tips are in order. First, midweek rates are a terrific bargain because, especially in winter, more people can travel on weekends. Second, innkeepers and their staffs are unending sources of information for anyone exploring an area or trying out a sport for the first time.

Here's to happy hunting!

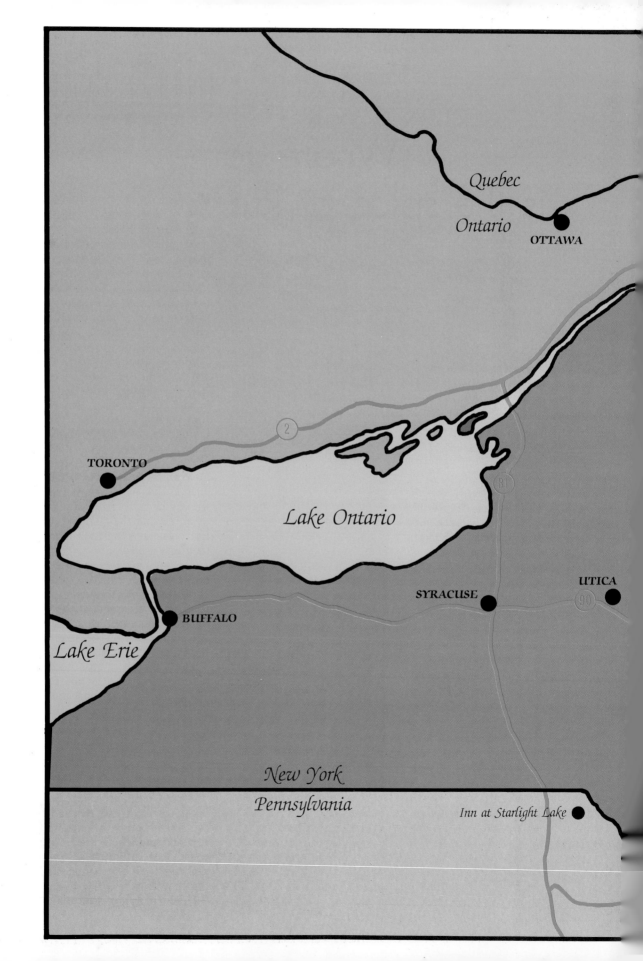

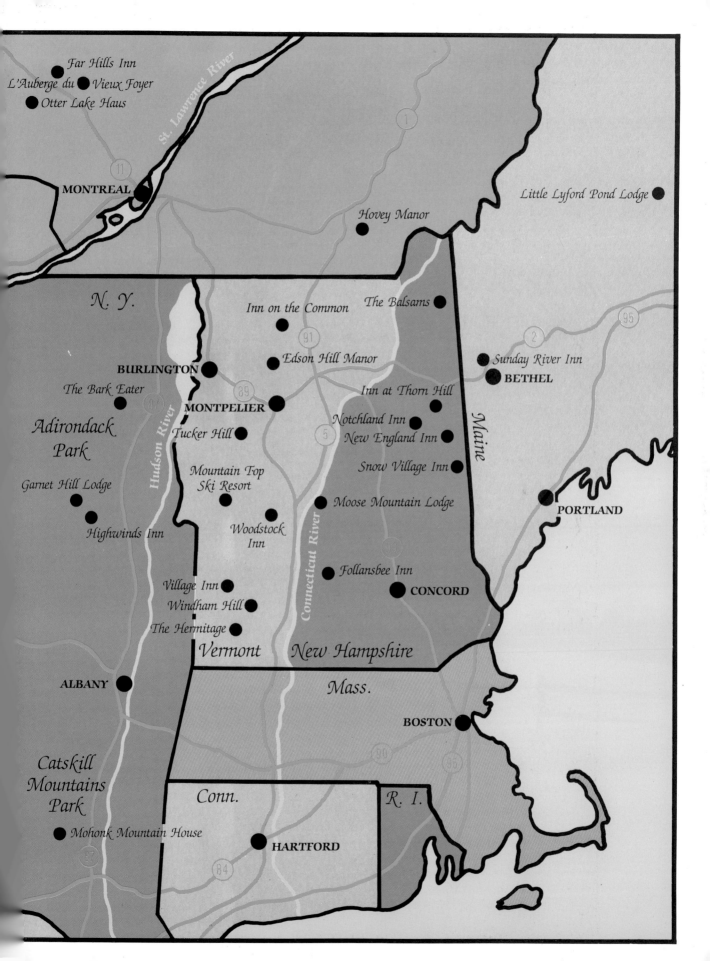

Far Hills Inn

L'Auberge du Vieux Foyer

Otter Lake Haus

St. Lawrence River

MONTREAL

11

Little Lyford Pond Lodge

Hovey Manor

1

95

N. Y.

Inn on the Common

The Balsams

91

Edson Hill Manor

2

Sunday River Inn

BETHEL

BURLINGTON

89

Inn at Thorn Hill

The Bark Eater

MONTPELIER

Notchland Inn

New England Inn

Adirondack Park

Tucker Hill

5

Hudson River

Snow Village Inn

Maine

Mountain Top Ski Resort

Garnet Hill Lodge

Moose Mountain Lodge

Highwinds Inn

Woodstock Inn

PORTLAND

Connecticut River

Follansbee Inn

87

Village Inn

CONCORD

Windham Hill

The Hermitage

Vermont   *New Hampshire*

Mass.

ALBANY

BOSTON

Catskill Mountains Park

90

95

Conn.

R. I.

Mohonk Mountain House

HARTFORD

87

84

VERMONT

INN ON THE COMMON

A picture postcard Vermont village

CRAFTSBURY COMMON, established in 1794, is a picture-postcard village with its central square, the "academy," which is now a high school, and a classic church spire, one of the most photographed in Vermont. The village sits benignly on the eastern shoulder of a glacial valley shared by the northward-meandering Black River and a number of good-sized farms. This gently rolling countryside of the Northeast Kingdom is less prosperous and less traveled than the rest of Vermont and perfect for cross country skiing.

Remoteness is a decided advantage, say innkeepers Penny and Michael Schmitt. Those who enjoy country inns will travel anywhere to find them, and being away from what Penny calls "the glitz" of the busier resorts guarantees a different kind of experience.

The "spiritual inspiration" behind the Schmitt's inn was a visit they made to a baronial home in Ireland in 1968. It was so memorable they began to think about opening an inn themselves. Five years later, while vacationing at their summer place, they saw an ad for the property and made their decision.

LEFT, the diversity of trails draws everyone from Elderhostel groups to competitors' training camps. BELOW and RIGHT, these photographs illustrate why innkeeper Penny Schmitt is able to say, "We fit the image most people have of the perfect country inn."

Like most of its neighbors, the original house dates from the early nineteenth century. In restoring it, the Schmitts melded a modern approach to interior design with a selection of handsome antiques carefully chosen to enhance each room. The coordination of colors, an original print or painting, and handcrafted quilts and rugs enhance every room of the house.

Two buildings of the same vintage have been added for additional bedrooms. The North Annex, newly refurbished, faces the common. The South Annex, across the street, has a lounge where guests can choose from a VCR library of 200 films and a kitchen for making light snacks.

The Schmitts host the cocktail hour from 7:00 to 8:00 P.M. and introduce guests to activities of the season and the local countryside. The small and loyal

staff contribute to the feeling of contact with the local community. Meals are served "dinner party style," in a room where full-length windows bring the outdoors inside visually.

Penny has spent years experimenting with "nouvelle cuisine," and feels she has developed an unbeatable collection of recipes. Generally, the evening's choices are made from what the marketplace offers combined with locally raised products such as lamb and quail. In season there are fresh vegetables and herbs from their own and local gardens. Special dietary needs can be accommodated.

Most people are adventuresome when it comes to eating, Penny feels. And, Michael adds, they also appreciate good wines. They serve a good, modestly priced house wine with dinner. Guests can choose to opt out or select from higher grade categories chosen by Michael to complement the entrées.

"There is an extremely sophisticated kind of traveler seeking inns these days," says Michael. Theirs, they believe, fulfills the image most people have of the perfect country inn.

INN ON THE COMMON SKIING

The people who come to the Inn on the Common for cross country skiing really love the sport, says Penny. They ski for skiing's sake. She and Michael share their passion. They are veterans from "the old days" before the sport became fashionable, and they show their commitment by sharing operational costs at the Craftsbury Nordic Ski Center, where their guests ski without charge.

The Center lies a few miles away by car, but guests can ski to or from it on an intermediate level trail of about five kilometers. There are big, open meadows here and to the west Vermont's highest peaks—Camel's Hump, Mt. Mansfield, Spruce Peak, Madonna and White Face—pierce the skyline.

About forty kilometers of groomed and tracked trails wind through the woods and fields along Lake Hosmer, where the Center runs seasonal training camps in sculling and canoe racing. The Center staff has trained naturalists who conduct nature and birdwatching tours. Developing a feeling for the woods is a nice way to approach the sport, Penny believes.

Another sixty kilometers of wilderness skiing is nearby, although some of it, for example the Bailey-Hazen Military Road is for experts only. But even a moderate skier can handle the tour of about twenty-five kilometers in the Lowell Range, according to Center director John Broadhead.

Everyone from Elderhostel groups to racers attending coaching clinics is drawn to the Center, which has equipment rentals and qualified instructors.

LEFT, each bedroom is individually decorated, but this has to be one of the most inviting. RIGHT, Craftsbury Common is one of Vermont's most photographed villages because of its purity of line and color as exemplified in the 1820 Congregational church shown here. Alfred Hitchcock's "The Trouble with Harry" was filmed in the village.

EDSON HILL MANOR

Like a house party in a private chalet

AFTER the steep climb from the mountain road the French provincial style stone-and-log building that sits on the brow of the hill gives the impression of having inadvertently driven straight to Canada. Stowe Village, with the hustle of its shops, restaurants, and alpine hype, could be a thousand miles away.

Originally, Edson Hill Manor was the indulgence of a wealthy gentleman who hired a series of prominent architects to build the ideal country estate. Its fame, however, lies as much in the doing as in the conception. The hewn beams in the living room were once part of a barn belonging to Ira and Ethan Allen of Burlington, principals in Vermont's early history. A former Burlington hotel contributed its brick walls; fireplace tiles came from Holland and brass, from Williamsburg. A local smithy crafted much of the hardware, and a fellow townsman spent one summer shaving the exterior logs of the manor walls with a broadax.

Once inside, guests feel as if they are in their own private chalet; having other people there only makes it seem like a house party. The resident hosts are Larry Heath, Jr., and his sister-in-law, Anita, who provide the right combination of cheerful assistance and benign neglect. The manor began when Larry's father, Laurence, Sr., who was devoted to skiing, brought the whole family to Stowe to live in the early 1950s. It became their home as well as an inn.

The main common room with its inviting fireplace, French windows, comfortable divans, and book-lined shelves

LEFT, French provincial influences are evident in the architectural style of the manor, which was chosen in 1980 for the filming of "The Four Seasons." The ski touring center, RIGHT, is converted from part of the riding stable, which offers alternative recreation in winter.

EDSON HILL MANOR SKIING

Stowe didn't earn its self-acclaimed designation as the Ski Capital of the East for nothing. It now receives the same accolades for cross country skiing.

Edson Hill Manor has forty-five kilometers of marked trails outside its doors. It is also part of a cooperative ticket system linking four other ski touring centers in the area, with a total of 180 kilometers of skiing.

Guests can go out the door and onto the trails if they choose. The Touring Center, located below the manor, is converted from part of the stable. Instruction and rentals are available.

The Edson Hill trails are marked by moderate climbs through mainly hardwood growth with frequent scenic views and the intermittent appearance of farms and second homes which assures that civilization is nearby. While most of the trails will appeal to beginner and intermediate skiers, there are some advanced wilderness trails in the system as well.

The family's favorite is the Old Billings Road and West Hill trails, which pass through the deserted homesteads and farms that once comprised the hill community of Mansfield. It later melded with the more prosperous village of Stowe. The Catamount Trail, its final link with the northernmost part of the state awaiting completion, comes directly into the Edson Hill system. Other wilderness trails, for example to Bolton Valley and westward over Smugglers Notch, will also tempt the expert skier.

makes a companionable gathering place. Pine paneling and fireplaces in several of the bedrooms contribute to the feeling of luxury, as do original paintings and prints.

The dining room, part of a more recent addition to the manor, takes full advantage of the 30-mile vista from Edson Hill. Only at night do a few winking lights reveal the "real world." On the lower level, a bar/lounge with an excellent sound system offers a lively atmosphere. Here, hot dishes like soup and chili are served at lunchtime.

The chef at Edson Hill is a personality unto himself. The sign of his creativity is reflected in the printed menu, which lists "veal du jour," for example, with the day's style of preparation dependent upon his mood. There always are several choices in meat, fish, chicken, and vegetarian meals, along with similar variety in appetizers and desserts.

Edson Hill Manor has additional sleeping accommodations in the Carriage House and the Annex, and while both are more modern in style, they still offer magical fireplaces.

Fishermen will be frustrated because the Manor's ponds are icebound in winter. The stables have a few horses for riding; in summer this becomes one of the principal attractions along with the terraced swimming pool and putting green.

BELOW, the tiled fireplace in the common room is the master design for others in the main house. Cordials and hot beverages are served while guests relax here with board games. RIGHT, Larry and Janka Heath are part of the second generation of innkeepers who make Edson Hill seem like visiting a private country estate.

TUCKER HILL LODGE

Vermont's Restaurateur of-the-Year

VERMONT is not among the places that first comes to mind when thinking about searching for buried treasure. Yet a small book published in 1970 lists Waitsfield as one of several sites where secret caches and even gold digging are part of its folklore. Surely the real discovery to be made here today is Tucker Hill Lodge.

Zeke and Emily Church haven't exactly tried to keep the place a secret; rather, over the past decade they have let the business build steadily on the basis of solid performance. Their philosophy is simple. They want guests to enjoy themselves, and they run the inn as the kind of place where they would choose to stay. Zeke's selection as 1985 Vermont Restaurateur of the Year attests to their success.

A CIA-controlled plot in the kitchen (Culinary Institute of America, that is) might overtake the world, if only the world could be accommodated at the inn. The dinner menus change daily and everything begins with absolutely fresh ingredients, an advantage of being situated close to sources of supply. Fresh fish is available daily from Boston, and in the growing season, vegetables, herbs, berries, and other fruit come from their own or local gardens.

Finding such a high calibre of food at an inn of this size, however, is quite surprising. Reading a week's menus makes a gourmand's mouth water. At least eight entrées are listed every night, preceded

Innkeepers Zeke and Emily Church, RIGHT, have established high levels of expectation of comfort, dining, and service. The peace and serenity of the natural setting, LEFT, are enhanced indoors by traditional country décor.

by a choice of two soups and four appetizers, which also change daily. With salad and dessert, this qualifies as a five-course European dinner. Zeke has also assembled a fine wine cellar of which he is rightly proud.

Waitsfield visitors caught up for one reason or another in the condominium/chalet scene, regularly check first with Tucker Hill Lodge to be sure they can have dinner every night before they reserve their accommodations. And the country breakfast will send guests out for exercise.

Other qualities contribute to the inn's success as well. There is the warmth of pine-paneled walls throughout the common rooms and many of the bedrooms. An immediate sense of comfort prevails from the welcoming fireplace in the living-room and the bowl of fresh fruit on the front desk to the sloping ceilings, old-fashioned wallpaper, and simple furnishings in the rooms.

A small bar on the level beneath the dining room with an interesting corner fireplace and old farm tools for decoration offers potential space for "whooping it up." Yet most of the lodge guests, whatever their age, seem to recognize a good thing when they've found it and merely concentrate on the peace, serenity and exceptional food—with just enough skiing thrown in to pique the appetite.

TUCKER HILL LODGE SKIING

Tucker Hill Lodge and its touring center are nestled on a ridge scarcely a stone's throw from Mill Brook, which tumbles down from the Appalachian Gap and meets the Mad River about a mile away in the village. The trails range along the ridge behind the inn, alternately passing through towering pines and hardwoods. Frequent views of the countryside to the west include Mt. Ellen and Lincoln Peak; both are around 4000 feet in altitude. Later, a working sugarhouse is a popular target in the springtime.

Most of the trails are intermediate level, with short loops for real beginners. However, most of the system can be managed after only a short time on skis. A section of more challenging terrain links with the Sugarbush Ski Touring Center. Also for the experienced is the Catamount Trail, part of which passes through Tucker Hill's network.

Qualified instruction is available and groups are accommodated, but individuals pace themselves. Fruit, snacks and something warming like soup or chili are available for light lunches at the touring center every day.

Diversions include the Sugarbush and Mad River alpine centers, plus sleigh rides, skating and shopping in the village. In the off-season, Zeke and Emily encourage canoeing and bicycling, in addition to standard sporting pursuits.

RIGHT, TOP, travel writers have been driven to find new superlatives to describe Tucker Hill's cuisine—a combination of classic and new American. BOTTOM, a corner fireplace and barnwood paneling contribute to the informal atmosphere of the bar. BELOW, one of the picturesque scenes waiting to be explored along the inn's trails.

MOUNTAIN TOP CROSS COUNTRY SKI RESORT

A family inn with lots to do

I F SOMEONE set out to design the perfect setting for cross country skiing, it would be hard to equal the wide, sloping meadows of the Mountain Top Inn at Chittenden, Vt. Behind the inn, a wooded peak shelters the network of trails from the prevailing westerlies, and below lies a frozen lake rimmed by mountains that create vistas in every direction.

From inside the inn, the spectacular view is best seen from a double-story window encasing the staircase between the main level and the dining room downstairs. Even the massive fieldstone fireplace in the living room can't compete for attention, unless it's after dark, for the eye is drawn constantly to the out-of-doors.

Eating has to be considered recreation in any season. Here, the dining room has a European feeling, its pastel shades of wallpaper making a pleasant complement to the natural colors of the wood interior. Light but comfortable Canadian snowshoe chairs, elm-framed with webbed seats, add an interesting touch. The menu is extensive and unashamedly American. Lighter entrées and vegetarian choices are included and special dietary needs are accommodated.

The Inn's proximity to Killington and Pico Peak ski centers probably accounts for the unusual appeal for of "crossover" skiers, those who want both downhill and cross country skiing. The downhill types are apt to be up and out early, eager to get the most from their day tickets. Cross country skiers are a more leisurely lot, since all they have to do is step out the door. They also can be first back in the afternoon to enjoy the sauna or the cocktail lounge.

For those who don't ski or who need a day of rest, a big, horse-drawn sleigh comes by the door regularly to take guests on a circuit through part of the Inn's thousand acres. Limousine service also

LEFT, the spectacular view from the double-story staircase window. BELOW, the inn sprawls across the horizon, while inside, RIGHT, a delectable dinner is served elegantly at a fireside table.

Non-skiers can choose ice skating...

or tobogganing...

or relaxing...

can be arranged for shopping trips to nearby Rutland.

The Lakeview Room on the main floor is a haven for reading or quiet conversation; another has a TV set with movie cassettes available; downstairs is a game room. Within view of the dining room, a small skating rink offers more visual entertainment.

Whether good innkeepers are born or made may be a moot question here. William P. Wolfe and his sister, Barbara McLaughlin, now share with their spouses, Jan and Bud, the innkeeping duties carried on since the 1940s by their parents, Bill and Margery. They're proud of their heritage, conscious of the inn's place in local history, and eager to share it all with their guests.

MOUNTAIN TOP SKI TOURING CENTER

Under the direction of Don Cochrane, former U.S. world biathlon competitor, the Center has expanded to 110 kilometers of well-designed and integrated trails, a third of them groomed and set with dual tracks.

The top of the mountain is almost 200 feet higher than the Inn, which lies at 2000 feet above sea level. The climb is rewarded by great views, a warming hut

with deck for picnicking, and terrain to match any ability on the way down.

One trail off the top leads to open meadows perfect for practicing telemarking and, indeed, the trails generally are wide enough to permit its use frequently. Both short and long trails swing back through the woods to the inn. The growth here is primarily hardwoods, which let in the light and allow for great views of the neighboring mountains.

Directly in front of the inn, a number of trails, including one for beginners, lead to the Chittenden Reservoir, 500 feet below. For the more experienced, there is a 20-kilometer loop around the lake, or trails into the adjacent Green Mountain National Forest. Another wilderness test, the Catamount Trail, which eventually will extend all across the spine of Vermont, also hooks into Mountain Top's trails.

In the spring, the working sugar house, another of the warming huts, becomes an especially popular destination. The third hut is located on the lakeshore.

The Center has a full staff of experienced instructors, equipment for sale or rent, a snack bar and a pot-bellied stove surrounded by benches, the ultimate in warming huts.

RIGHT, staff in the ski shop poses amid the cross country ski equipment. BELOW, the setting sun dramatically guides the weary skier homeward.

WOODSTOCK INN

A complete winter resort since 1892

NEW ENGLAND is filled with historic places. But not many villages exhibit their sense of the past as well as Woodstock, Vermont. The colonial homes clustered around its famous, ship-shaped common, called "The Green," the churches with their Paul Revere bells, and other evocative buildings are only the visual part of the story. Beneath the surface beauty lies a lively awareness among villagers of their heritage.

Since this was the site for the first rope tow put into operation in the United States in 1934, it was predictable that Woodstock would develop into one of the most complete ski resorts in the country. The old Woodstock Inn had begun advertising for winter business when it opened in 1892, although people came then mostly to snowshoe, skate, and sleighride. Long a summering place for the wealthy, the village fostered skiing even before the sport had two styles and two names. Once the "ski-way," or lift, revolutionized the sport, winter was changed forever in New England.

Woodstock's famous sons and daughters are legion, but the most interesting for cross country skiing buffs probably would be George Perkins Marsh, whose 1864 book, *Man and Nature*, sparked the modern conservation movement. A University of Vermont professor who eventually became ambassador to Turkey, Marsh learned about man's capacity to alter his environment from his father. He observed from their farm on Mt. Tom that the overharvesting of timber caused devastation on the hills surrounding them.

The Marsh farm became part of the Frederick Billings estate, and a daughter of the Billings family married Laurance Rockefeller, a leading force in present conservation circles. It was he who established the modern Woodstock Inn, built

LEFT, skiers can walk to the trails on Mt. Tom via the covered bridge, one of four in the area, or to the touring center, located on the inn golf course, BOTTOM. The Woodstock Green and inn, RIGHT, where travelers have been accommodated since the eighteenth century.

LEFT, *the common room's massive stone fireplace, decorated with folk art.* RIGHT, *the formal dining room, with some of its elaborate cuisine set out in a buffet.*

in 1969 and formerly part of the Rockresorts group.

Although the colonial style, white brick building which sits back from the Common is in keeping with the architectural spirit of its neighbors, this inn has all the accoutrements of a modern hotel. A striking fieldstone fireplace greets visitors in the main common room, which is flanked by an informal coffee shop and a cocktail lounge. A more formal atmosphere holds in the main dining room, where guests are required to dress for dinner.

All skiing facilities are free to those registered for midweek specials or the Inn's Seniors on Snow program. An indoor sports center opening in 1986 with pool, exercise rooms, racquet sports, and saunas, will complete the Inn's recreational opportunities.

The village has an historic library, a theater, and an array of shops and dining places. Nearby are covered bridges (two right in town), the famous gorge of the Ottauquechee River, and the Vermont Institute of Natural Sciences.

which are groomed and tracked. By far, the majority are rated intermediate.

Beginners can practice on the level terrain of the golf course. More advanced skiers will want to try the trails that wind around the sides of Mt. Peg to the east with its cloak of evergreens.

On the other side of the village, also within walking distance of the inn, are the carriage roads and meadows of the Rockefeller estate on Mt. Tom. They climb from the village's 700-foot elevation to 1400 feet above sea level through mixed hardwoods and conifers that offer views of the countryside.

An ungroomed trail connects from the top with Suicide Six, Woodstock's alpine center, where the second rope tow in the U.S. was erected in the thirties. Another test nearby for those who like wilderness skiing is the Skyline Trail, not part of the Center, reputed to be the first one cut for cross country skiing in the state.

The Touring Center has expert instructors, a full ski shop, tours, movies, and a restaurant.

WOODSTOCK INN SKIING

God and the glaciers left just enough room in the valley behind the inn for an 18-hole golf course that converts in winter to the headquarters for the Woodstock Ski Touring Center. Professional forester John Wiggin, the Center director, has been responsible for laying out the seventy-five kilometers of trails, about half of

LEFT, *easy chairs in clustered groupings create conversation areas in the main common room.*

VILLAGE INN

Where the untracked woods are best

THE NAME Landgrove doesn't always appear on road maps . . . and that is fine with most of its residents. They've even resisted having the town highways hardtopped, partly to slow down the speedsters from the city who regularly invade the Manchester-Stratton area. After winding along the few miles from the main route turn-off, the inn appears like the sight of an oasis.

The Snyder family got into the inn business because they love skiing. Don and Elsie, the first generation of owners, had brought their children to this part of Vermont from their New Jersey home every winter for years. A friend there had a cousin at Landgrove with a farm to sell and in the late fifties the inn was born. Although the parents still keep a watchful eye from their new home nearby, the inn is primarily the responsibility of son Jay and his wife Kathy.

Don is a trained landscape architect, but his real love is carpentry, and much of the character of the place reflects his interest. It was a treat for him to have the time to make the necessary renovations when they bought the place. The living room, for instance, was worn down to the subfloor. The wide, red spruce planking he found to replace it came from the top of Stratton Mountain when they were clearing trees for the ski development.

LEFT, the original farmhouse has been incorporated with former outbuildings to make a spacious inn all under one roof. In the main activity room, BOTTOM, couches are drawn up before the fireplace at one end, with the bar and game tables at the other. RIGHT, one of the comfortable guest rooms.

LEFT, red spruce floor-boards in the living room came from the top of nearby Stratton Mountain. The hot tub, RIGHT, doubles as a solarium.

The inn had previously been a children's camp. Renovations resulted in the Rafter Room Lounge, a game room and bar located in what was a former barn used for activities. Full-length couches arranged before an impressive fireplace are an irresistable magnet, especially after a day outdoors.

Two more modern additions in an attached wing lie at right angles to the lounge. The bedrooms here are more conventional, except that the ones in the second story over the present children's game room and hot tub spa have acquired the same kind of cozy feeling that Don and Elsie achieved in the old part of the house.

Lighted paddle tennis courts are available all year round as well as skating on the small pond, snowshoeing and tobogganing. A neighbor hires out his team for sleigh rides, too.

Because the inn has two plexiplave tennis courts, a heated swimming pool, and a pitch-and-putt golf course out the back door, it is the center of some local social activities in summer. But generally, this is a place for withdrawing from the hectic pace of the outside world.

If a new word could be created, it would be "unpace," translated meaning, "to slow down and set one's own formula for relaxing." The countryside, the feeling of removal from the outside world, and the easy attitude of the Snyder family provide the essential ingredients.

VILLAGE INN AT LANDGROVE SKIING

Even though he's not a native, Don has a Vermonter's laissez-faire attitude about skiing. He believes that skiers will find their own terrain, whether they prefer cross country or downhill. Once they find what they like, they'll return to it. Beyond that, he says, with a firm shake of the chin, "real cross country skiers don't want tracks set for them!" Therefore, the skiing at the inn is woods skiing, tracked by skiers only.

Since the inn faces the Hapgood Recreation Area, one of the most popular parts of the Green Mountain National Forest, this is a compatible mix. There is open land next to the inn for absolute beginners and easy trails on their and neighboring land where neophytes can acquire their ski legs.

For longer excursions, there is the Utley Brook trail, popular with intermediate skiers, a steady, moderate climb with a rewarding, downhill return that is about a ten-kilometer round trip. Side trails on the sides of Peru Peak, Styles Peak and Mad Tom Notch will challenge the better skiers.

Guests and day skiers are required to register their skiing destinations at the inn. Several commercial touring centers can be found in the nearby area, where the Snyders are happy to refer those who want grooming, tracking, and instruction.

WINDHAM HILL INN

A ski "learning center" with comfort and style

LEFT, country living with style is shared generously with guests by innkeepers Ken and Linda Busteed. BELOW, the former milk house is now the ski shop. RIGHT, instructor/guide Jon Tobey helps a beginner learn how to balance on skis without the help of poles.

THE NEXT BEST thing to owning an elegant place in the country would be to make frequent visits to Windham Hill Inn. Ken and Linda Busteed have transformed this typical Vermont farmhouse, circa 1825, into a home that exudes comfort and grace.

The spacious, four-chimneyed house sits at the end of its own lane. It has a substantial look, reflecting the prosperous family farm that once flourished on this hillside above the West River Valley. Although operated as an inn for many years, the house was in poor physical shape when the Busteeds bought it in 1982. It was the perfect challenge for Linda, a trained professional interior designer.

Every room has a distinct personality, yet each melds with the whole. Linda has combined pieces they found in the house with furnishings of their own and additions found in area antique shops. The house holds at least a hundred individual signatures of her talent, from books, prints, and quilts to the single frame of an old sleigh mounted on one of the dining room walls.

Most captivating is Linda's collection of high-buttoned shoes. She uses them imaginatively, some so cleverly placed they evoke the feeling that their wearers might still be standing in them.

Guests gather for drinks before dinner in "the wicker room," an airy common room—almost a solarium—with windows covering two sides, high rafters and a European stove. The view of low, wooded hills rimming the horizon contributes to the coziness of the place, outside as well as inside. The more formal "front parlor," which has a fireplace, and another small sitting room with a covered stove are ideal for clusters of conversation among more intimate groups.

Linda is as creative in the culinary arts as she is in decorating. Only inn guests are served and, when the house count is low, everyone sits at a single, large table. Separate tables are optional, but dining here is similar to attending a private dinner party where hosts share the serving duties.

Part of their pleasure derives from watching their guests interact and in observing the inn's "buffering capacity," as Ken calls it. Boston think-tank types min-

gle with people they might never otherwise meet, notes this former health-care industry executive.

The Busteeds recently bought the old barn that was part of the original farm and have converted part of it to interesting sleeping accommodations with sweeping views. A charming library nook stocked with marvelous old books invites browsing. Chamber music and theater-in-the-round presentations occupy the unused open space in summer. Down in the Valley, recently designated a state scenic corridor, guests can explore the longest covered bridge in the state, as well as a plethora of shops and restaurants.

WINDHAM HILL INN SKIING

The Busteeds prefer to call their place a "learning center." Surely they have an advantage in the presence of their instructor/guide, Jon Tobey, who has done as much as anyone in the state of Vermont to promote cross country skiing. Jon, who formerly ran his own touring center, loves to teach, guiding first-timers along until they can make extended trips into the woods.

The few kilometers of packed trails laid out in the woods and fields surrounding the inn are ideal for practicing. Their names are delightful—Buck Rubbins, Hurry Back, and Raven's Ridge. The network tracked in the meadow, called Folsom's Mowings, is fun too. Where cows once grazed and hay was once mown, people wearing skinny skis now spend hours tracing huge figure eights in the snow. The owls and hawks on the hillside must be amused at the sight.

A few miles above the inn is Tater Hill Touring Center, which has thirty kilometers of what Jon considers excellent trails. Three other equally fine commercial touring centers are within twenty miles.

Eight kilometers of flat to gently rolling trails lie between the West River and Route 30 in the valley. Guests can ski to lunch at the village café. A few miles west is Jamaica State Park, also untracked, where an excursion of near equal distance follows the bed of the defunct West River Railroad, dubbed "36 miles of trouble." Jon also gives guided tours on wilderness roads with scenic views in the nearby countryside.

Land that was a prosperous farm in the nineteenth century is now a recreation area. The inn buildings can be seen in the distance.

From ski trails to wine cellar, a cornucopia of things to do

THE HERMITAGE

THERE'S a five-ring circus going on at The Hermitage Inn. Sometimes innkeeper Jim McGovern is ringmaster, and at other times he's part of the show. In addition to his duties as host, Jim is an oenophile, breeder of rare birds and hunting dogs, shooter, guide, art collector, maple syrup maker, and skiing promoter.

The amount of activity at The Hermitage is difficult to encapsulate. On a given day, cross country devotees bustle past the windows on their way to ski; visitors flow in and out for a meal or a stop at the wine cellar; and someone comes by for a guided shooting excursion. Jim presides over it all with great aplomb.

The Hermitage retains the spirit of its beginnings as a working farm in the 1870s. The husbanding is just more selective these days. More recently a private vacation retreat, the place has operated as an inn since the sixties. Jim took over the business in 1971, after working as a carpenter and at other resort jobs in this part of Vermont.

He has expanded the inn from four rooms and a 40-seat dining room to twenty-nine rooms and an addition at the rear of the main building which seats 200. The French doors and windows are as appealing by day as the high-ceilinged room is by candlelight at night. Primarily, the reputation of the inn's continental cuisine makes it one of the most popular eating places in the Mount Snow–Wilmington area.

The accolade Jim prizes most is from "Wine Spectator," probably the leading publication in the wine business. In 1983, he received its Grand Award for restaurant wine lists, one of only forty-two in existence, recognition of the breadth and depth of his cellar, an inventory of over 25,000 bottles and 1000 labels. Circulating among the guests tables at night, he offers suggestions for just the right wine to complement their meals.

LEFT, innkeeper Jim McGovern in the wine cellar, for which he won a prestigious national award. Jim's advice on wines is most helpful at dinner. RIGHT, inn guest rooms are filled with antiques.

Jim reveals his other passions more freely. Signed and numbered Delacroix prints adorn the dining room walls. Soon after buying the inn, Jim began assembling a complete collection of the 116 prints in the French artist's series, of which he has 102.

Throughout the inn some of his hundreds of duck decoys are on display, handcrafted items also of considerable value. Like the wines, "these are not collected," he says, but definitely are for sale (except, perhaps, for a few).

The decoys are a natural adjunct to his love for shooting. He has at least a dozen English setters at any one time, which he breeds for show and hunting, and about sixty species of game birds. The latter appear on the inn tables or are sold to other restaurants. Some are released for hunting in the private preserve he supervises, a 900-acre parcel of wooded terrain whose trails are used by cross country skiers in winter.

THE HERMITAGE INN SKIING

Cross country skiing has progressed says Jim, since the early seventies, when they offered free fondue if people would just put on these silly skis. No longer are they "opposite people," as he terms it, who pursue alpine or nordic. Now everybody does both.

The Hermitage Ski Touring Center operates from the annex of the inn, which sits on a low ridge at the foot of Haystack Mountain. The trails adjacent to the inn lie on relatively flat terrain, covered by towering conifers and hardwoods. As they climb the ridges on both sides of the access road from Route 100, the trails become more challenging. Of the seventy kilometers of groomed and tracked trails, less than half are rated advanced.

For the hardcore skier, the new Ridge Trail, three and a half miles of wilderness skiing between Haystack and Mount Snow, is the alternative. The inn books lift tickets which can be used for the first part of the trip to the top of either alpine center. Norpine equipment is required, and tours can be arranged. Jim promises great views from Brattleboro on the east to Bennington in the west and the lakes country in between.

The Ridge is also the locale for an annual racing event held in March. The center conducts other citizen races as well during the season. Jim sponsors a racing team for NASTAR-style events at Mount Snow.

An experienced staff is prepared to handle every level of ability and to teach the latest techniques.

Everyone from beginning skiers, BELOW, to those seeking rugged wilderness trails, ABOVE LEFT, can be accommodated at the touring center. RIGHT, the dining room, where memorable dinners are served to guests and public.

NEW HAMPSHIRE

INN AT THORN HILL

Jackson, where skiing is *the* way of life

SOME PLACES have a certain magic about them. Jackson, New Hampshire is one. This is a real mountain town, where people ski to work and guests ski from inn to inn for lunch or entertainment. The maze of trails that encircles this village symbolizes the residents' commitment to the sport.

The tradition of hospitality goes back to the early nineteenth century when artists and writers, drawn by the region's spectacular scenery, were put up in local farmhouses. Since then, Jackson has adapted to the changing times, as first trains then cars made their impact. Likewise, skiing moved from the pioneering days before the turn of this century through its mechanical revolution.

The community's indefinable quality partially influenced Bob and Pattie Guindon to buy the Inn at Thorn Hill. The principal motivation, though, was their affinity for the inn itself, a Victorian mansion designed by Stanford White. As Pattie says, "Something happens when the right person comes to the right inn."

Within ten days after first having seen it, they had signed the papers. Neither will soon forget their first two months. They jumped in cold with a month remaining in the winter season and followed that with a solid month of renovations. They remodeled rooms, added baths, painted, plastered, and hung 196 rolls of wallpaper.

The interiors retain the Victorian style. The main common room, with its fireplace and a magnificent vista of seven of the Presidential peaks, has a formal arrangement of furniture from the Guinons' former living and dining rooms. A small

LEFT, the inn, originally designed as a private residence by Stanford White, looks as solid as the White Mountains rising around it. RIGHT, part of the extensive network of touring trails that makes Jackson one of the prime ski towns in the country passes by the inn door.

sitting room off the vestibule is cozy and informal; full-length swinging doors separate it from the bar. The dining room extends across the back of the inn, its pastel green and pink color scheme attractive by candlelight and even more striking in daylight, with its view of nearby wooded hills.

The bedrooms are roomy, nicely appointed, and most of all comfortable. Those in the house are furnished entirely with antiques, while those in the Carriage House and cottages lean more toward the contemporary. The Carriage House also has a living room with fireplace. There's an activity room downstairs in the main house.

Guests returning from skiing, which begins at the door, find that hot mulled cider and hors d'oeuvres await them. Serving outside diners permits the inn to carry a very full menu supervised by a first-rate chef. Dining here completes the overall experience.

Pattie loves "the winter people," as she calls them. The majority of their guests are cross country skiers, "energetic, enthusiastic, happy people who come prepared to entertain themselves," she says. The older guests, some into their seventies, amaze her most. "They want an early reservation at dinner," she laughs, "but they're first in for breakfast and then it's up and out—usually all day long!"

INN AT THORN HILL SKIING

The Jackson Ski Touring Foundation, established in 1972, maintains one of the finest trail systems in the northeastern U.S. The range of skiing is a magnet for cross country skiers.

Seventy kilometers of groomed and tracked trails meander through the woodlands, meadows, golf courses, stream beds, and lakeshores surrounding the village, which sits in a cluster of low mountains at the approach to Pinkham Notch. The network is designed to qualify for major competitions, which the Foundation hosts each year. Another seventy kilometers of wilderness skiing is part of the JSTF system, of which forty-six kilometers are for strong skiers only.

One of the favorite trails with average skiers, Pattie reports, follows the course of the Ellis River on its way down from the Notch. Many guests make the round

trip, 7.7 kilometers each way, stopping for lunch at Dana Place at the far end. Others prefer to be dropped off there by car for the long glide back to town.

More challenging terrain can be found on the sixty kilometers of Appalachian Mountain Club trails in the Notch. Wildcat Mountain Ski Center, which also welcomes telemarkers, is the starting point for an 18-kilometer trail that drops 3245 feet from the summit to the village.

Nearly ninety property owners allow their land to be used by the JSTF, asking only that skiers stick to the trails and do not litter. The Foundation also has a special permit for using White Mountain National Forest Land.

The staff, under director Thom Perkins, spends eleven months a year on trail work, constantly widening and smoothing in the off-season so that they can provide superior skiing under any conditions.

RIGHT, a common room and a guest room give some idea of the antique furnishings throughout the inn. BELOW, desserts are a specialty of the menu.

THE BALSAMS

A grand hotel, with ski trails at the doorstep

THE BALSAMS is one of the grand old hotels developed in the nineteenth century, when a summer holiday meant a month or two spent in the mountains or at the shore. Few have survived the decades following World War II, when the American love affair with the automobile also spurred an addiction for motels. Travelers are again cultivating an appreciation for luxurious surroundings, unlimited service, and playing fields on the premises.

It hardly seems possible that a hotel of 200-plus rooms can invoke the personal quality of a small inn, but the proof lies in a stay at The Balsams. The magic quotient is the direct, daily involvement by innkeepers Steve Barba and Warren Pearson. "The guests own the inn," says Warren, "we just run it for them."

Before taking guests to their room, the bellman gives an introductory description of the common rooms, the dining room card, the evening's movie and other social activities, if it's a midweek stay. In the rooms fresh fruit, a bottle of The Balsams' maple syrup, and the day's paper await.

Echoes of the hotel's past are visible in closets with built-in drawers, marble baths, and beautifully preserved furnishings. But the bedrooms are more agreeably modern than any motel room, updated with constant refurbishing.

The original part of the inn is an extension of the modest, clapboard hotel built in 1873. It houses the T-shaped dining room and two floors of public rooms. These consist of lounges with live entertainment, large and small sitting rooms with fireplaces and an occasional TV, and a conference room where Dixville Notch voters gain national attention every presidential year by being the first to register their votes.

The success of the Balsams attests to the pride of the people of this region, where catering to travelers is a century-old tradition. Nearby Colebrook was once the wealthiest town per capita in the state. Concerned local people persuaded Neil Tillotson, a successful Yankee entrepreneur who hailed from the commu-

LEFT, "Grand Resort Hotel" is the label correctly applied by the Balsams' management. A chef, BOTTOM, discusses with the dining room staff the evening's entrées, which are exhibited for guests' perusal as they enter the dining room. RIGHT, the Library, one of several gathering places.

nity, to buy the 15,000-acre property when the hotel was failing. He persuaded two young staffers to take it over in the 1970s and within five years, Steve and Warren had revitalized the operation.

They now lease it with a third partner, who is also executive chef. Not only are these three aware of what their guests want, but they have also initiated some of the recent innovations that are transforming hotel travel in the 1980s.

THE BALSAMS SKIING

Guests at The Balsams can take their skis from the storage room downstairs and walk out the door or ride the shuttle bus to the lodge at the ski center. All facilities are available there for both downhill and cross country skiers.

The Balsams' trail map lists forty kilometers of tracked and groomed trails and forty kilometers of wilderness skiing. A loop near Lake Gloriette in front of the hotel and parts of the other trails are rated beginner level skiing. Many of those rated more difficult are manageable after only a short time on skis. Undoubtedly the most popular are the "Fox Trot Trail" and "Fox Trot Connection," which lie in wooded, slightly hilly terrain along the Mohawk River below the hotel.

From the 1850-foot elevation at The Balsams, trails climb a few hundred feet to the country club (golf course in summer) and wind around the side of that ridge to link with the Fox Trot. Behind the inn there is a 500-foot rise via the Reservoir Trail to the Mud Pond section,

which lies between Mount Abeniki and Sugar Hill. This is the beginning of the collection system for the hotel water supply and the stream that feeds the lake.

Other alternatives for skiers are wilderness trails, for which it is also necessary to register, and a "wild card," exchangeable at other downhill ski centers in the northern New Hampshire area.

Probably the highlight for most guests is viewing the videotape of their day on the slopes and trails back at the inn. Instructional? Perhaps not. Entertaining? Always.

NOTCHLAND INN

An inn restored to life with spirit and skill

LEFT, history, legend, and a superb natural setting meld with the ministries of the Bernardin family, who have performed major miracles in restoring the 120-year-old mansion. RIGHT, two of the charming guest rooms.

THE MOUNTAINS of New Hampshire, some which rise more than a mile high, were visible on clear days to voyagers arriving by ship to settle the New Land. They were called the Crystal Mountains then, for the tales of fabulous gems to be found in them. The first white man to climb Mt. Washington, Darby Field, sought a huge carbuncle reported to give off rays of light visible for miles. That was in 1642, only two decades after the Puritans landed.

Crystals of snow and ice comprise the fortunes of winter for modern explorers in the White Mountains. One of the few places where it's still possible to appreciate the wild beauty of this mountain landscape is The Notchland Inn, at the entrance to Crawford Notch.

For John and Pat Bernardin, the desire to restore the fine old granite and timber house, owned by one family for 103 years, superseded their plan to run an inn. The house had been boarded up, vandalized, and abandoned for six years when they found it. They invested two years of 16-hour days reviving it.

They stripped the place to its skeleton and rebuilt. They removed wood trim, numbered it, and replaced it intact; they installed baths, showers, and in some cases standing washbasins. The end result reflects an adherence to the integrity of the original architecture without an attempt to recreate a particular era.

Most of the bedrooms have fireplaces and, with their high ceilings and easy chairs, become spacious, uncluttered sitting rooms. A few others, smaller and more intimate, combine well as suites with shared baths.

The main dining room, actually the oldest part of the house, looks new, converted from the tavern that stood by the highway for decades. It now forms an L-shaped wing. Windows line both front and rear walls, and maple tables and chairs contribute to the cheerful atmosphere. A double fireplace makes an effec-

tive room divider. Outside, the skating pond, the sauna, and a few birches encroach only slightly upon the wall of trees that rises behind the inn.

Pat, who ran an executive dining room in Boston, concocts four-course gourmet meals with unruffled calm in a spacious kitchen. John and their son Christopher share the serving duties.

THE NOTCHLAND INN SKIING

There are only about 800 acres of private land left in Crawford Notch, and the Bernardin family owns half of it. John has opened up twenty kilometers of groomed trails and another ten tracked by skiing only which run along the Saco River opposite Route 302 and on Nancy Mountain behind the inn.

It's hard to imagine that the section on the river side was once cleared farm pastures and fields, although photographs at the inn prove it. The tall hardwoods that have reclaimed the land now provide shelter for perfect glade skiing. Once there, it's even harder to believe that a busy highway is nearby.

The trails wind through gently rolling terrain on the far side of the river and keep returning to it at scenic spots. John has utilized some national forest land, for which he has a special permit. Near the lower end, a ridge trail leads to another plateau with more easy skiing and excellent views.

The trails behind the inn provide a little more excitement for good skiers because of their sweeping descents. Only a fraction of the system is rated advanced, however. There are an additional ten kilometers of wilderness trails and John, who has twice competed in the Henley regatta, will take guests on guided tours.

There are many developed touring centers within easy driving distance.

The white birch first took over the fields where farm cattle once grazed. Now it's the cross country skiers.

NEW ENGLAND INN

Memorable experiences of all kinds, including a ghost

THE NEW ENGLAND INN is appropriately named, for it has the quintessential look of its region: clapboard buildings with clean lines set off by spanking fresh white paint and green trim. Appropriate, too, that it began life as the Samuel Bloodgood Farm and opened as an inn in 1809, one of the stops on the Concord Stage line through the already famous Washington Valley. During the heyday of summer-long stays in the mountains around the turn of the century, it was known as "Mountain Rest."

A different pace and energy infuse the place today, ingredients supplied mainly by innkeepers Joe and Linda Johnston. Long addicted to inn travel, they have searched this country and the world looking for ways to improve their business.

Joe and Linda take daily, personal interest in seeing that guests have a memorable experience, and their spirit is contagious. For instance, they hold "theme weekends," centered on a special activity or ethnic flavor. They've initiated "mystery weekends," complete with professional actors to carry off the whodunit.

The Johnstons particularly enjoy introducing their guests to cross country skiing. Linda can cite countless stories of converts, her supreme success being an older lady who'd never tried any kind of sport and who considered that learning to ski changed her life.

Although most guests come for winter sports, many simply want to relax in the pleasant atmosphere of the inn. The

LEFT, the front parlor decked out for Christmas, along with the outside, TOP. RIGHT, hearty New England fare goes a long way on a cold winter day.

somewhat formal main living room has an inviting fireplace and a wall of windows that make it cheery during the day. A smaller sitting room is a good place to escape with a book to read or a companion for a chat. A grand piano reigns in the "front parlor," where bookshelves harbor marvelous old, even rare, titles for perusal. Both these rooms have fireplaces as well.

The bedrooms in the main building, all recently redecorated and all with private baths, are roomy and furnished with big fourposters, accented by patterned quilts and matching curtains. Family style arrangements and single rooms are found in the cottages and log cabins.

Across the street is the Meetinghouse, a columned building with a charm of its own but more simply furnished, used mainly for conferences and overflow. Clyde, the inn's resident ghost, lives there too, but as an old employee makes his presence known only in the staff rooms.

Hearty and delicious New England fare is featured in the spacious dining room, which also has a fireplace. Because both the inn and the bar are open to outside guests, and because they have an imaginative chef, the Johnstons maintain a varied and frequently changing menu.

The inn is located a few hundred yards away from the main highway through the Washington Valley, which adds to the feeling of being "away from it all." Still, the North Conway shopping district, with its outlets and gift shops, is only a short distance away, should civilization be desired.

NEW ENGLAND INN SKIING

Alpine skiing once dominated the ski scene in the Mount Washington Valley, but no longer. Soon after buying the inn, Linda and Joe Johnston became interested in cross country skiing. Quickly, they recognized that the inclinations of its devotees were ideally suited to the country inn style. They established the Intervale Nordic Learning Center, a complete touring center located in the lower level of the Meetinghouse across the street from the inn.

Ideal trails for beginning skiers lie adjacent to the Center; they are popular for skiing to the bakery and a local pub for lunch or refreshments. Behind the inn at

the foot of Bartlett Mountain lies the major portion of the 40 kilometers of trails, all well-maintained and track set.

Short loops for skiers of beginning or moderate ability have been cut through woods dominated by birches close to the inn. Also for intermediate skiers are the trails that follow the East Branch River and then climb along the lower ridges of the mountain mainly through conifers until the hardwoods on the higher elevations are reached. The trail to the Outlook, rated intermediate, is well worth the effort.

The expert trails are longer routes, not groomed, that go over the mountain, one to another outlook area with a view of the valley and the Presidential range. Other national forest land trails in the region will test the experts, too, and maps can be obtained in the village. For variety, exchange ski privileges are available with other touring centers in the Valley.

The new skating techniques being taught at the Intervale Nordic Learning Center.

RIGHT, the inn, which first opened in 1809. BOTTOM, country prints and comforters warm the guest rooms. BELOW, a cross country version of Madonna and child.

SNOW VILLAGE INN

Where personality makes the difference

LEFT, guests continue to add to Pat Blymyer's collection of caps. RIGHT, every day should be started with a hearty breakfast.

U P THE HILL from the little hamlet of Snowville, Snowvillage Inn puts a modern fillip on enjoying winter. The setting is serene: a big, rambling house backed by towering pines and overlooking its own meadows and apple trees. The altitude is sufficient for one of the best views of the Presidential Range in the entire Mt. Washington Valley.

Inside, the place oozes personality. The living room is decorated with overstuffed furniture drawn up before a mammoth fireplace whose first function is to keep the grand piano in tune and its second, to warm the guests. An inner room serves as a staging place for drinks and convivial conversation, the latter often centered around the collection of visor caps that covers the ceiling.

The dining room wing has a European look, the influence of the former owner, who was Swiss. The unbroken view of the mountains tempts one to linger long over breakfast.

Each of the bedrooms has a distinctive character, too, a blend of design, compass direction, and furnishings. Everywhere there is a happy clutter of books, paintings, mementoes, photographs and soft sculpture.

Years of wandering in the movie business, she as a hairdresser and he as a gaffer, led Ginger and Pat Blymyer to the inn business. They tried running a foster children's home in Appalachia in the late sixties, and although they went broke, they discovered they enjoyed working together. Ginger's love of books was the catalyst. She liked Gladys Tabor's

descriptions of New England, and reading Elizabeth Goudge's *Pilgrim's Inn* gave her ideas about running one.

They began their search in 1978. Their choice, Snowvillage, matched an image Ginger had of an ideal location. Other associations with the house were right, too. For many years it had been the summer retreat of Frank H. Simonds, correspondent and author, who broadcast a nationwide radio program from here. Appropriately, the bedrooms are identified by authors' names.

Pat and Ginger continue their movie-making stints. Early on, it was the only way they could make the improvements they wanted. The previous innkeeper had let the business slide, and in their first year the Blymyers lost $49,000. Ginger called in the neighbors for a party to celebrate the fact that they hadn't lost $50,000.

Their daughter Tanya assumes the innkeeping duties when they are away. She describes the cuisine as "innovative," because they all like to cook and experiment. They serve a single entrée at dinner, but vegetarian meals and other dietary accommodations are available. Guests wander freely in and out of the kitchen, consulting, sniffing, and sampling. The number of returning guests attests to the quality of the meals.

SNOWVILLAGE INN SKIING

Gentle exercise is available in any season at Snowvillage. In winter, there are cross country trails, ideal for beginning and intermediate skiers. In other seasons, one of the trails doubles as an exercise trail, designed by a former guest.

The skier is seldom far from the lodge. The trail network uses the terrain on the hillside behind the inn extremely well. There are occasional scenic views, and circling the trails will give anyone a good workout.

The country road, not plowed beyond the inn in winter, offers a longer excursion, as does "No. 5, forever," which takes skiers through the woods and over a logging road and crosses two lakes on the return to Eaton Village, a few miles away. Skiers can either be picked up at the store there or ski home.

Foss Mountain, above the inn, is another wilderness trek. Those who hike, snowshoe, or ski to its 2000-foot summit are rewarded with full circular view.

The inn has a ski shop with instruction and rentals available. More ambitious skiers have a plethora of choices in commercial touring centers and alpine runs in the Mt. Washington Valley.

General views of the inn, including the dining room, RIGHT, which overlooks the Presidential Range of mountains.

MOOSE MOUNTAIN LODGE

A great place to be

"THINK SNOW"

LEFT, the view from the lodge extends across the Connecticut River Valley forty miles into Vermont. RIGHT, did early skiers have more fun?

BOTH PETER AND KAY Shumway grew up in skiing families, and they delight in helping people learn to enjoy the sport. Kay confesses that she loves the winter season best for the inn business. "Everyone comes in so cheerful after being outdoors," she says, "and no one thinks anything can be wrong with the world."

"Cross country skiing has given back to many people a reason for taking a winter holiday," says Peter, "those who either have reached an age when alpine skiing no longer appeals or who find it too expensive. And, a lot of younger people want to introduce their kids to the sport."

The Shumways bought Moose Mountain Lodge as a great place for themselves to live, not because they intended to run an inn. Perhaps that is why arriving guests immediately feel that they are being welcomed into the Shumways' home.

Kay presides in the big, airy kitchen with superb calm amidst guests wandering through to the ski shop or helping themselves to an ever ready supply of cookies and other goodies. Peter shows up frequently, as his outside duties permit, to fix a fire, share office duties, or chat with guests about skiing.

The lodge was built in the late thirties when nearby Dartmouth College students and their friends were discovering the marvels of the new uphill transportation for skiing. The logs and stones which were cleared from the hillside to make way for the ski slope went into the construction of the lodge. The rustic style awakens memories of ski train outings among skiers of that "vintage."

Outside diners are not accepted at the lodge, and Kay admits she does resent it a bit when their guests decide to go out for dinner. They like the interaction that takes place around the single long table, where the guests often sit talking by candlelight until 10 or 11 P.M. Kay prepares a single entrée for dinner with choices of appetizers and vegetables. Seconds on her delicious dessert concoctions can be arranged. The only other rule for guests, after complete relaxation, is that they must eat well, seldom a problem after a day spent in the fresh air.

Entertainment is low key, usually provided by guests and friends.

From the lodge's 1600-foot elevation there is an unbroken view southwestward thirty-five to forty miles to Killington and Mt. Ellen in Vermont's Green Mountains. The road climbs rapidly from Lebanon, a thousand feet below in the Connecticut River Valley, and the last hill to the lodge can be difficult in certain weather conditions. An accommodating neighbor permits guest parking, then Peter shuttles them to the lodge.

All this contributes to what Kay calls "beautiful isolation." Many guests come just to enjoy that, content to curl up by the huge fireplace in the living room or to settle for a game of cards or ping pong in the downstairs playroom.

MOOSE MOUNTAIN LODGE SKIING

There hasn't been a moose seen on Moose Mountain for some time, but guests at the lodge will share the trails there with plenty of birds and small game. For beginners, easy trails are just a short ski from the lodge around the beaver pond. More challenging trails have been opened up on the ridge behind, requiring a steep initial climb.

About thirty-five kilometers of trails are packed out by Peter's crew on snowshoes and skis. In addition, guests can hook into real wilderness skiing on the Appalachian Trail and the Dartmouth Outing Club trails, all about a mile away on the mountain.

The six-mile Ridge Trail traverses the mountain in another direction and has great vistas. Pleasant tours on old logging and abandoned town roads are also nearby.

The former ski tow slope is perfect for learning or practicing telemark skiing, and first-rate alpine centers are within easy driving distance. Instruction is available, and the Shumways insist that guides be arranged for wilderness trips.

In general, they want guests to be able to learn to ski, to advance if they know something about it, or to exert yet not overextend themselves during their visit to Moose Mountain.

RIGHT, ceiling beams, big windows, and an inviting fireplace make the main common room a pleasant place to relax. Kay and Pete Shumway, BOTTOM, enjoying themselves as usual. BELOW, rustic beds, some fashioned by hand by Kay, are used throughout the inn.

Try Our Hot Cider,
or Hot Spiced Kir!
Appetizers:
Seafood Crepes $4.95
French Escargot Soup $2.25
Marinated Artichokes $3.50
Entrees:
Veal Piccata $13.95
Swordfish $12.95
Boneless Prime Rib $14.95
Roast Duckling $14.95
Enhance your meal with
a special bottle of wine

Remember Homemade Desserts

Everyone is ignorant —
only on different subjects.

FOLLANSBEE INN

Ski trails in maple sugar country

ABOVE, the inn at Christmas time. TOP LEFT, the friendly trails at Follansbee. BOTTOM, the menu on the dining room chalkboard; at least one item changes daily.

THE WORLD once traveled directly past the doors of the Follansbee Inn. Now, the main highway and the interstate lie down the road a bit, leaving the tiny hamlet of North Sutton to a quieter life. It is a typical country crossroad, with only a combination grocery store/gas station and the 1794 Baptist Church to keep the inn company.

Removed by time more than distance from the busy Lake Sunapee region, the inn has endured the chameleon changes of any structure that has survived since 1840, when it was built as a farmhouse. For some, the interiors, particularly the bedrooms, evoke memories of stays at a family summer place, as it should, since the inn sits on the shores of Kezar Lake.

Midwesterners Dick and Sandy Reilein wanted a lifestyle as well as a career change when they bought the inn a couple of years ago. As newcomers, they were relieved that the chef who'd been at the inn was willing to stay. He in turn was delighted with their ideas for expanding the menu.

Even drop-in dinner guests should have a dining experience, Dick believes, rather than just "going out to eat." The food is

LEFT, innkeepers Dick and Sandy Reilein, in a relaxed moment, and Dick checking out the trails, RIGHT.

good country fare with seasonal appetizers, homemade bread, salads, and three or four entrées daily including fish and beef. The menu changes regularly, and special requests are accommodated. Dick also has considerably expanded the wine list.

The only coercion guests have to contend with is the family-style breakfast, which the Reileins prepare themselves. Juice, coffee, and Sandy's famous granola are set out on the sideboard, and guests wander into the kitchen to order their hot food, usually a single special dish which Sandy concocts. It's a gentle way to get guests mingling, but at night they all return to their individual tables.

Sandy has worked miracles with her imaginative use of antiques, found in the outbuildings and basement of the inn and in neighborhood shops. Schoolhouse desks, old books, and some of her teddy bear collection (started long before the current craze) alter the perspective of the wide, high-ceilinged hallways upstairs. A pair of "spectacles" on a desk near the entrance, the roomboard from the inn's early days, and framed quotations about inn travel add whimsical touches.

The low-ceilinged room that served as the tavern when this was a wayside inn is now a cozy sitting room, but something of the old atmosphere clings to the very rafters. The present bar, with its attractive fireplace, is another gathering place across the hall adjacent to the dining room. Television and telephones are absent. The Reileins have also established a no smoking policy that has been well received.

FOLLANSBEE INN SKIING

Easy skiing is accessible out the front door of the inn, either around the shores of Kezar Lake or in nearby Wadleigh State Park on trails opened up by snowmobiles. A seven-mile trail with more challenging terrain and great overlooks of the valley and Mt. Kearsarge is reachable from here, too. In spring, guests observe the maple sugaring operation on the farm through which the trail runs.

A short drive away is a commercial touring center with forty-five kilometers of groomed trails. There are scads of hiking trails and logging roads in the area to explore (which are not groomed), and maps are available in nearby New London shops.

Other choices include the well-known alpine centers, Mt. Sunapee and King Ridge, which limit the number of daily tickets sold to avoid lift lines. Inn guests can reserve ahead for theirs.

Non-skiers may try a walk around the lake road with its views of several decades of styles in vacation homes. Skating and sleighrides are also available nearby.

NEW YORK
AND PENNSYLVANIA

HIGHWINDS INN

Superb Adirondack views and trails

A VERY REMARKABLE MOUNTAIN were the words that labeled it on the first surveyors' map in 1779. Located on a gap left unsurveyed in the early land grants, it acquired the name Gore from local usage. In the report of the state's first official topographical survey a century later, Verplanck Colvin affirmed that the remarkable thing about Gore was that no one had ever been able to find its summit because of the "intricate group of peaks of which this mountain was composed."

Thousands of skiers ride lifts to one of Gore's summits these days unaware that on the other side of the mountain lies one of the two sources of industrial garnet in the United States. Even before Colvin's report was published, the Barton family began the mining operation that still bears its name.

The Bartons built a home there in 1933 for the present generations of the family to use in summer and winter. That home is High Winds, altitude 2500 feet above tide. Although production was suspended at this site in 1983, the processing buildings remain and a number of the staff houses still are occupied. Above it all sits the house with its unbroken view of Adirondack wilderness.

Very few publicly maintained roads go as high as the one from North River, a hamlet on the shore of the Upper Hudson, to the inn. It rises 1500 feet in five miles.

PREVIOUS PAGES, a magnificent vista of the Adirondacks from Highwinds, which retains its original atmosphere as a family retreat, RIGHT.

(Guests can be met at the store in the village if driving conditions are difficult.) Once having reached the inn, a sense of total isolation prevails.

Because the house is small, it's inevitable that guests will feel like its temporary owners. The rooms are furnished with an understated elegance that encourages such fantasy. The inn is still too young to have acquired the air of a public place. Indeed, it may never.

The guiding spirits behind opening the inn to skiers were Peter Barton and Jim Nash, who represent the family business interests here now. Garnet is still mined at another location, oddly enough called Ruby Mountain.

Kim Repscha is innkeeper, chef, and general factotum. She describes her cuisine as "country French," with everything made from scratch, including homemade breads and desserts. A small number of outside diners can be accommodated by reservation.

Generally, however, tranquillity reigns as Kim, with her gracious manner, serves dinner by candlelight. Afterward, guests settle into quiet conversation by the fireplace, which is constructed of garnet bound in hornblende. There are a game room and hot tub downstairs.

It's pleasant at evening's end to step outside, where the mountains are a bowl of stars undiminished by light. Peter claims they have "the most spectacular sunsets in the Adirondacks." With such a backdrop, it's easy to believe.

HIGH WINDS SKIING

The Bartons influenced the earliest development of downhill skiing at Gore. There, the first open slopes and tow were constructed adjacent to North Creek village in the thirties. C. Rodman Barton, grandson of the company's founder, built a tow on "Pete Gay Hill" near the mines and also devised the idea of busing skiers from the village to this side of the mountain from which they could ski back down. "Ride Up, Slide Down" became part of the lingo of the eager crowds riding the ski trains from Albany and New York.

Inn guests use parts of those trails and the inactive mining access roads for sport today. The groomed trails are only about ten kilometers in extent, but they go to scenic spots like The Vly, a small lake, and overlooks on the mountain. Behind the inn is the huge open mine pit cut through cliffs that develop dramatic ice formations in the course of the winter.

Possibly the most interesting trek is the connection with Gore Mt. Ski Center, where telemark skiers can purchase a lift ticket and spend the day. Others will return by the cross country trail. The views of the Adirondack High Peaks to the north are superb. From the inn, it's a climb of nearby a thousand feet, but worthwhile for the return run.

In the other direction, the trails connect with the Garnet Hill Ski Touring Center and, beyond that, the Siamese Ponds Wilderness Area. Other unpacked trails are located on state land nearby. Guides can be arranged.

All in all, this is an alpine setting which is rare in the east.

The stuffed black bear is a relic of the Adirondack wilderness, along with the centuries-old log, LEFT, ABOVE, that provided the sidetable in the living room. RIGHT, guests can ski to the summit of Gore Mountain, or, via inn trails, to both developed and untracked skiing.

THE BARK EATER

Olympic expertise at your disposal

WINTER was not kind to the Algonquin Indians, the original bark eaters. Its rigors reputedly forced them to boil the bark and roots of trees to survive, a practice which earned them the derision of their southern cousins, the Iroquois, who coined the term. Although the native Americans preferred snowshoes, they probably would have taken to this modern madness.

If they spent much time with Joe Pete Wilson they would certainly come to enjoy the frolic. Although he is six feet tall and muscular, once those narrow boards are hooked to his feet, he turns into an animated child. His wife Harley matches his enthusiasm, but she must serve as the anchor to windward, keeping the inn operating on an even keel.

The inn itself is a comfortable old farmhouse, built in the early 1800s. Stagecoaches once rolled past the door on the main route to Lake Placid. Depending on its owner and the cooking skills of the owner's wife, this often served as a way station. The evidence lies in the house, initially a classic, two-story, four-room building typical of the region, where the Wilson family, owners since the 1940s, found birchbark used as insulation.

The house underwent transitions during the nineteenth century. First, a big dining room with an overhead dormitory was added for community-style sleeping to accommodate travelers. Next, a smaller "front room" was built, with bedrooms above, evidently in wintertime when travel

LEFT, the dining room, with its cobblestone fireplace, is a gathering place at any time of day at The Bark Eater. RIGHT, innkeepers provide the magic ingredient at each place; here Harley and Joe Pete Wilson with their apprentice, daughter Katie.

was slow, for the floors don't quite match and the fireplace was constructed entirely indoors. More bedrooms were added on the opposite side of the original house, as well. Eventually, a porch across the front unified the whole.

Harley and Joe Pete have made attractive renovations in most of the upper-level rooms where coordinated quilts, comforters, and curtains meld with the family pieces and other antiques they've acquired. Given Joe Pete's passion for collecting, the place is quickly turning into a small museum.

A log cabin, built by the family, sits on the edge of a wooded plateau a short distance from the farmhouse and not far from a mountain stream. This has bedrooms on two levels, each with a sitting room warmed by a standing fireplace.

The gathering place at this inn, however, is the dining room, part of which is adjacent to the kitchen in the old part of the house. Soup, salad, and a single entrée (with adjustments for dietary needs) are the rule, and Harley's recipes have become collectors' items. Hot drinks, soup, and quick lunches are available in season, and, of course, big breakfasts.

Joe Pete, a former Olympic and world class competitor in skiing, biathlon and bobsledding, author and well-known raconteur, believes he should project a more sedate image at dinner with his guests. But everyone soon learns that he is mischievous at heart.

THE BARK EATER SKIING

Standing on the overlook of the Ridge Trail at The Bark Eater, one can almost envision the path of the glaciers that left their imprint on these ancient mountains some 10,000 years ago. To the west are Cascade, Porter, and Pitchoff mountains, and on the northwest, the Sentinel Range. One can actually watch snowstorms moving over them into the valley where the inn lies.

The trails here glide from sheltered spruce and balsam growth to open meadows to the hardwoods that claim the upper reaches of the surrounding hills. All are suitable for intermediate skiers (sidestepping and running out into the trees is always permissible for the less adept). Beginners may want to practice

for a while on the level ground in front of the inn and in the pastures where the horses graze in summer.

The Bark Eater sits at the edge of New York State's prime wilderness area, the High Peaks, and the neighboring Sentinel Range wilderness area. Less than thirty miles away are the trails surrounding the St. Regis Canoe Area. The entire Adirondack Forest Preserve is laced with wilderness trails.

Probably more popular in winter are the Olympic nordic trails at Mt. Van Hoevenberg, part of the facilities used for Lake Placid's 1980 Winter Games. Fifty kilometers of groomed and tracked trails are fun for amateurs as well as challenging for competitive skiers. Bobsled and luge races nearby occasionally divert attention. Ice-skating on the outdoor oval in the village plus hockey and skating events at the Olympic Center offer evening entertainment.

The inn is a comfortable old farmhouse, with some rural amenities, ABOVE. The nearby Mt. Van Hoevenberg Olympic Recreation Area, TOP RIGHT, provides winter excitement of all kinds, while more relaxed skiing, BOTTOM, is found on the snowy meadows of the Bark Eater.

A breathtaking location and great skiing

GARNET HILL LODGE

UP IN THE Adirondacks, skiers have replaced the legendary lumbermen on the wood roads, and white water rafters float down the Hudson River where the spring run-off once carried logs to the mills. While new traditions are made, one old one, good innkeeping, is upheld by George and Mary Heim at Garnet Hill Lodge.

The location is breathtaking, an eyrie perched above Thirteenth Lake, which is dramatic even when frozen over and great for skiing. The surrounding mountains seem low, but the lake elevation is 1674 feet above sea level and the main lodge is 200 to 300 feet higher.

The Log House is the center of inn life. A thirty- by seventy-foot structure, it has a long, open, raftered room at its heart and sleeping accommodations above. The Heims have made some changes. They have added an extention to the front with a sun porch whose windows capture the lake view and, overhead, enlarged bedrooms with porches, picture windows, and full-length glass doors. All the rooms have baths. The decor could be termed modern rustic, for it fits the image of a hunting and fishing lodge.

A deep garnet fireplace dominates the large common room. Couches made from hewn logs and easy chairs by the fire are occupied at almost any time of day. Guests read, chat, or nap there, before, after, or instead of exercise. The common room is also a strategic place to savor aromas from the kitchen around the corner. Youngsters can play pool or ping pong nearby, and a small library at the far end offers quiet space.

Tables for dining are arranged opposite the fireplace area and, in busy periods, guests sit on the sun porch as well. Garnet Hill food is an attraction for vacationers and second home owners nearby, in addition to local folk.

Her experience entertaining as a Navy wife and her store of exotic recipes from countries where they lived and traveled made Mary's transition to innkeeping a smooth one. They have meat, fish, chicken, and vegetarian choices every day, along with a special feature, fresh-baked rolls, and desserts. They offer hearty breakfasts and lunches, and the Saturday night buffets are extraordinary.

LEFT, Garnet Hill Lodge occupies its own mountain top in the midst of the six-million-acre Adirondack Park. The touring center is the hub of the largest privately-maintained trail system in the region, and links with surrounding wilderness areas. RIGHT, the ski shop.

The inn's Saturday night buffets are famous.

Garnet Hill's other accommodations lie down the hill from the lodge and have different characteristics. The Birches is a recent addition with modern furnishings, set right in the woods. Staying at the Ski Haus, where the touring center is located, is like visiting a friend's cabin.

Most interesting is Big Shanty, the former home of the Hooper family, who owned the garnet mine around which this small settlement developed in the last century. It, too, has a big fireplace and the unmistakable air of a long history of colorful events.

GARNET HILL LODGE SKIING

Garnet Hill Ski Touring Center maintains the most extensive network of privately-operated trails in the Adirondack region. Beyond it is the access to untold miles of wilderness skiing. Not far away, Gore Mountain Ski Center welcomes telemark skiers. With a fully-equipped shop, experienced instructors, and videotaping capability, Garnet Hill has a pretty unbeatable combination.

Most of the fifty kilometers of groomed trails, of which twenty kilometers are tracked, lie on the long ridge behind the lodge. Intertwining loops will entertain those of moderate ability, and a few will raise the pulse beat of better skiers. A small area is lighted for night skiing. Beginners have the choice of short trails around the Ski Haus and those along the shore and surface of Thirteenth Lake.

The ridge trails move from wooded areas to scenic views of the Adirondack High Peaks. Longer and more challenging runs extend from five to ten kilometers back down the ridge to cross traveled roads where skiers can be picked up by the center's shuttle bus.

For experienced skiers, there are untracked trails to the abandoned garnet mine, to Hour and Puffer ponds, and into the Siamese Ponds Wilderness Area, over 100,000 acres accessible on foot only.

Probably the most popular is the all-day tour from the top of Gore Mountain, led by touring center director Dick Carlson or his staff. This traverses challenging terrain that includes a couple of lakes and exceptional views.

TOP RIGHT, perfectly groomed and tracked trails, and, BOTTOM, a perfect ending to a day. LEFT, one end of the main common room is given over to pool, ping pong, and board games.

MOHONK MOUNTAIN HOUSE

A continuous campaign against boredom

LEFT, skiing and skating are only a step away from the front verandah. BELOW, portraits of the co-founder Albert Smiley and his wife, Eliza, hang in the "parlor."

AT MOHONK, the word is re-creation, part of the Smiley family's philosophy for generations. Alfred Smiley discovered this spectacular setting with its gem of a lake on a family outing in 1869. He persuaded his twin brother Albert to invest with him in the small inn operating there, and in 1870 a legacy was begun.

Winter's mantle of snow and ice makes the place more magical than in summer. Carriage trails and footpaths beckon the cross country skier. Skaters head toward the frozen lake. The golf course has a perfect hill for tubing.

High-ceilinged bedrooms, many with fireplaces, have magnificent views. On one side they face the lake with the mountain rising behind it, and on the other, a panorama of the Rondout Valley and the Catskill Mountains.

The common rooms are reminiscent of a day when vacationing was elegant. Tea is served every afternoon in the "library," which is surrounded by windows and French doors leading to verandas overlooking the lake. The "parlor" above doubles as a theater with a twelve-foot-square screen and seating for 225 people.

The ceiling in the main dining room is three stories high, and the fireplace arch measures six by three feet. A smaller dining room is used for lunch and for all meals if the midweek attendance is slim. Mohonk's corridors are a museum in themselves, four floors of paintings and prints ranging from landscapes by Hudson River School artists, to religious subjects, to old political cartoons.

A modern fitness center and sauna are tucked away on a lower level. The recreation staff wages a continuous battle against boredom, with daily indoor and outdoor events encompassing all ages and interests. Paddle tennis is one alternative, for example. There are small sitting rooms for viewing TV or playing board games, one of which has a piano.

Mohonk is famous for its study programs and seminars devoted to such topics as languages, computer courses, and current issues. It's believed that the "mystery weekend" idea originated here in the late 1970s, an innovation now widely copied. In its present version at Mohonk, a renowned mystery writer prepares a slide presentation that is shown to guests. The winning team is guaranteed a reservation for the next mystery weekend. a free return visit.

The entire staff is experienced and personable. This is the kind of place where the waitress or waiter remembers a guest's dietary preferences after the first meal, and the bellman asks about the day's skiing.

This mountain is part of the Shawangunk range that rises abruptly a few miles west of the Hudson River, north of New York City. The lake elevation is 1247 feet and Sky Top, the peak, is 1542 feet. Its physical location intensifies the feeling of isolation.

LEFT, the food is bountiful and quiet nooks for relaxing are plenteous at Mohonk. RIGHT, Mohonk is dedicated to the Smiley family philosophy that contact with the natural environment is essential for humankind

MOHONK MOUNTAIN HOUSE SKIING

The amount of energy generated by outdoor sports enthusiasts at Mohonk is

impressive. In winter, cross country skiers ramble through trails used in other seasons for horseback riding, hiking, and carriage driving. Forty kilometers of groomed and tracked trails, fifteen of them rated advanced, knit the mountain top together.

Despite its rugged looking facade, Mohonk has a remarkably varied terrain. Leaving the hotel on one side of the lake, there is a gentle climb along the western ridge on a trail with spectacular overlooks. Others wind along the side of the mountain.

Opposite the hotel, a short, stiff opening section begins the climb to the summit trails or to long loops on the far side of the peak and beyond to the ridge above the gate house. The trail that circles Sky Top runs through giant hardwoods and pines past breathtaking views of the summit escarpments. Wooden benches offer respites at particularly scenic spots.

The preserve that the Smiley family maintains surrounding the mountain and similar protected land behind it offers another 200 kilometers of wilderness skiing. Guests can arrange for guides and picnic lunches.

Magnificent as the views are from indoors, it's only emerging from the hotel that one can truly appreciate the beauty of the natural world.

THE INN AT STARLIGHT LAKE

A good place for beginners

LEFT, the inn has expanded by incorporating parts of the verandah, here shown during the Christmas season. The food varies between continental and American cuisine, with mushrooms applying to either, BELOW.

THE DELAWARE River drops downward from the Catskills near the northeastern Pennsylvania border, bumps into the Moosic Range of the Appalachians, and begins its southerly course to the Atlantic. Not far from where the river becomes the border with New York state sits a well-preserved, dowager lady of nearly eighty years. The Inn at Starlight Lake has presided over the transition from the days when summer brought guests who pursued sedate exercise to today's shorter-term winter jaunts where guests spend their days romping through the wilderness on skis.

The latest change in style was the idea of Jack and Judy McMahon, who bought the inn in 1974. Two years later growing public as well as personal interest in cross country skiing convinced them to remain open winters. The response and their trail system have grown ever since. That is not surprising, for here is an ideal combination: trails at the doorstep and deep comfort of the kind that makes leaving the launching pad difficult.

"The Blessing of the House is Contentment" reads a sampler in the main common room, surrounded on one side by easy chairs around a fireplace and, on the other by a standing fireplace and rockers. Upstairs are bedrooms with a pleasant mix of styles, "what was here" combined with modern necessities.

More people are taking winter vacations, the McMahons observe, and vacation homes like those around the lake (which pre-date the inn) are being winterized. The Inn dining room has become a beacon, primarily for its food, but also for its pleasant ambience. Windows admit

THE INN AT STARLIGHT LAKE SKIING

The word for the trail network at Starlight Lake is expansive. This is due not only to its extent but even more to the countryside through which it passes. Behind the inn, the access is a brisk climb along the hillside that encloses the lake on the western side. About midway is an old quarry from which was mined the bluestone slate used on the streets of New York and the walkways at the inn.

From the lake, at about 1300 feet elevation, to Top of the World, at nearly 1800 feet, and over the ridge to Perch Pond, there are changing views of the surrounding farmland and low mountains. Opposite the inn the trails wind similarly around the ridge that separates Starlight Lake from another even higher lake. The trails crisscross through partly wooded, partly open terrain.

Of the groomed trails, only five out of thirty kilometers are rated advanced. Of the tracked trails, twenty kilometers are considered beginner and five, intermediate. An additional five kilometers of wilderness trails are available, rated intermediate.

In general, this is companionable skiing. Among the choices are short or long trips into the village for lunch. There are longer treks past places like "Nip Your Nose Rocks" and "Yes, You Can," which will test the best skier's mettle.

The touring center at Starlight Inn offers something satisfying for those wanting a good workout and an exhilarating treat for anyone trying the sport for the first time.

sun most of the day; an enclosed portion of the former front veranda overlooks the lake; and hanging plants and old fixtures add warmth and personality.

The inn has an extensive cuisine, another reason why it attracts outside diners. It is particularly pleasant to relax in the intimate atmosphere that holds when the house count is low. Next to the dining room is a bar/lounge and, just around the corner in the living room, a grand piano where the McMahons do, on occasion, reveal hidden talents.

Both Jack and Judy came from careers in the theater to the inn business, which they consider an extension of the entertainment world. Jack, from Chicago, performed as a singer in night clubs, light opera, and touring companies before settling in New York City, where he eventually became administrator of Mercury Records. Judy, also from Chicago, studied speech and drama, spending one year at the Yale School of Drama. She and Jack met while both were performing in an off-Broadway production of "John Brown's Body."

Their venture into the inn business was "the challenge of a lifetime," says Jack, for the house was in poor condition. Through sheer persistence, they set a failing business on its feet even while raising four children.

Among the "perks" of a visit to Starlight Lake are the McMahons' impressive record collection, open to use, and a priceless store of classic, 16-mm films, which guests regularly enjoy.

RIGHT, innkeepers Judy and Jack McMahon can be persuaded to draw upon their theater backgrounds to entertain the guests on occasion.

MAINE

SUNDAY RIVER INN

A dandy system of trails adjacent to the inn

PREVIOUS PAGES and LEFT, the inn is nestled in the lower reaches of the Mahoosuc Range in Maine's western mountains. Built originally to house Alpine skiers coming to the ski center "up the road," the inn now attracts mainly cross country skiers.

EVEN longtime Maine-iacs have trouble discerning whether innkeeper Steve Wight is a native. His dry humor is characteristic of that made famous by dozens of writers from and about this state. The treatment is gentle, to be sure; it is definitely part of the warmth with which he and his wife Peggy surround their guests.

Steve describes himself as "first generation out of the woods and trying to get back" when he returned from Vietnam in 1970 after five years in the Air Force. He and Peggy had met working at a resort in the Bethel area, and they agreed that Maine was where they wanted to spend their lives. Fortuitously, they found that friends who owned the inn needed a manager.

Buying the inn in 1971 was what Steve calls a "faith move," for they had neither funds nor experience. What they did have was community support. The fact that Steve's father had grown up in Bethel and his grandfather had been a guide in the Rangeley Lakes district was the key.

Today the Wights have a family-run and family-oriented inn, unpretentious and comfortable. The living room extends across one end of the building, with a fireplace on one side and two walls of windows that overlook the deck and the open expanse where the trails begin. Views of woods and hills nearby give the bedrooms overhead a cozy air. All share dormitory-style bathrooms.

A fireplace at the far end of the dining room adds warmth to interesting decor. Tables and chairs of knotty pine, work of a local craftsman, have unusual bases fashioned from retrieved machine parts. An addition in the rear accommodates groups and overflow in busy times.

An open kitchen is sandwiched between the two main common rooms, and meals are served buffet-style from the front counter. It is hearty, home-cooked fare, usually a single entrée with choice of vegetables, equal to the demands of those who spend the day outdoors.

The odor of fresh bread and baking desserts draws people inside in late afternoon for the evening social hour hosted by Steve and Peggy. They always have dinner with their guests and are around during the evening, unless they have a community commitment. Steve is a member of the Bethel board of selectmen, and both of them are involved in church work.

Occasionally, a guest may find their style a bit too informal, but generally even the most uptight slowly begin to relax. The Wights run the kind of place where people can be themselves. The camaraderie that develops, with a little coaching from Steve and Peggy, is something special.

Steve says he likes the psychology of cross country skiers because they are open to learning about an area. Within easy driving distance are story-filled towns with names like Paris and Norway. In Norway, Artmeus Ward, Maine's best-known contribution to early American humor, learned the printer's trade. Perhaps there's something in the air up there.

SUNDAY RIVER INN SKIING

In a state where the chickadee is the official bird, the white pine, the state tree, and "I Guide," the state motto, Sunday River Inn Ski Touring Center encompasses it all. The first two reside on the system of trails adjacent to the inn, along with animal tracks and an occasional glimpse of wildlife. Steve and his staff provide the guiding.

The touring center has twelve kilometers of groomed trails and twenty kilometers of tracked trails on old farm and logging roads, some of which climb the long ridge beside the inn. For a mild challenge and picturesque landscape, there is the trail that follows the Sunday River. Even inexperienced skiers can enjoy the longer trip to the Artists' Covered Bridge downstream, terminus of the annual ski and canoe race that traditionally ends the winter season.

Extensive choices for hardier skiers invite exploration with the help of Steve or his staff. It is exciting just to hear him describe some of the landscape they invade, such as the Mahoosuc Notch, up the Sunday River valley.

The first range of the White Mountain National Forest rises southwest of Bethel. Most exciting are the trails in Grafton Notch State Park to the north. This is the heart of the range that sends the Androscoggin River from its outlet in the Rangeley Lakes to New Hampshire before it turns back toward Maine, flowing through the broad valley near the inn on its run to the sea.

In short, for beginner or expert, the skiing here is serendipitous.

The inn was the first commercial location chosen by Elderhostel International for its seminars, conducted regularly by innkeepers Steve and Peggy Witt. BOTTOM RIGHT, Steve leads a tour from the Artists' Covered Bridge, called the most photographed in Maine.

LITTLE LYFORD POND LODGE

Getting there is half the fun

LITTLE LYFORD Pond is definitely one of those places where getting there is half the fun. Taking off from Folsom's Air Service Base at Greenville, Maine, one then learns why Moosehead Lake, with its 350-mile shoreline, is considered the greatest of all New England lakes. More than a thousand feet above sea level, it stretches for thirty-five miles toward Canada, bounded on all sides by mountains and other small lakes.

The plane soon turns east and, after a short ride, drops its passengers at Lyford II, about ten minutes on skis from the lodge on Lyford I. Guests also ski in from Greenville, twenty kilometers away, or from a traveled road about twelve kilometers distant. Although baggage can be brought by plane, it's advisable to pare down personal necessities to what can be taken in a good-sized pack.

Once at Little Lyford, nothing matters except enjoying a wilderness experience made comfortable by people who know backcountry living yet who cherish such fillips as gourmet cooking and fine wine. Joel and Lucy Frantzman are prepared to cater to guests to a point. But for the most part, the attraction here lies in things enjoyed independently.

The cabins, for instance, offer seclusion. They are worlds unto themselves, fragrant with the smell of logs used in their construction and the smoke from the woodstove. The rooms are warm and cozy, especially inviting after a day of skiing. The beds are comfortable, and each has both blankets and a sleeping bag.

In the morning, it takes minutes to revive the banked fire. One's ablutions come from water heated on the stove. It's salubrious, living so simply, and yet so comfortably. Those who choose Little Lyford also choose no running water,

Individual cabins with sweet-smelling pine interiors, gas lights, and wood stoves make ideal retreats. Each has its own stockpile of wood, BELOW. In winter, guests ski or fly into the lodge, UPPER RIGHT.

Beginners can ski right around the lodge and on the two ponds, or they can venture beyond.

Mountains with names like Elephant, Indian, Baker, and White Cap rise all around, providing only backdrop for some treks, but a target for more proficient skiers. There are open slopes for the telemark skier, for instance. Wilderness cabins can be destinations, too, as rest stops for a picnic lunch or for overnight stays.

The shorter trail used for access from the outside is an easy one that follows the west branch of the Pleasant River most of the way. Nearby on Mount Katahdin, the Appalachian Trail begins, or ends. In the other direction along the river, a popular tour of about seven kilometers goes to Gulf Hagus Gorge, called Maine's Grand Canyon.

Small game, birds, deer, and moose are visible on the trails. Beaver dams often form the frozen surfaces over which skiers pass.

Since the land is still owned by the timber companies, signs of logging are prevalent. No operations are near enough to the lodge to spoil the unbroken stillness and beauty.

The Frantzmans frequently ski with guests, especially if they feel there is any uncertainty about using the trails.

outdoor toilets, and taking care of their own house chores.

There are compensations in addition to the beauty, the serenity, and the great skiing. Platform tennis and a sauna are two alternatives. The main cabin has an equally inviting stove around which to chat or to share the day's events before dinner. Shelves lined with books provide evening entertainment, unless someone organizes a board game or charades.

According to Joel and Lucy, their guests tend to be vigorous, those who "think young even if they're not young." But there are almost no age limits. They come to be quiet, to enjoy the out-of-doors and to relish the relaxation this complete isolation engenders.

Joel's cooking certainly contributes to the contentment. He enjoys experimenting and chooses from an eclectic collection of recipes as his mood, or his palate, moves him. He must be up to the mark, because the air alone stimulates appetites.

LITTLE LYFORD POND LODGE SKIING

Eighty kilometers of marked and tracked trails through woods and over frozen lakes surround Little Lyford Lodge. Joel advises guests each day which trails are best to use given their abilities and the prevailing conditions. Square markers indicate the routes leading away from the lodge and diamond-shaped ones, those returning.

Doing research for this book was not an unwelcome assignment for consultant Joe Pete Wilson and writer Marge Lamy, ABOVE LEFT, shown on the trail at Little Lyford. Left, the Frantzmans' son Seth has to settle for adult playmates part of the time. RIGHT, the main cabin and outbuildings viewed from the ridge where the sleeping cabins are built.

CANADA

HOVEY MANOR

George Washington's home amid Canadian snows

THE BOOKS on the shelves that line the walls of the main salon at Hovey Manor tell a quiet story about the life of this lovely old home and reflect its various owners. While a fire crackles nearby, it's soothing to absorb the feeling of the passing time and events that have mellowed these rooms.

North Hatley and the other small towns around Lake Massawippi have remained a small pocket of English incursion into the prevailing French culture of the Eastern Townships. The town was settled at the beginning of the nineteenth century by British immigrants and United Empire Loyalists who left the colonies after the Revolution. One of the land grantees and North Hatley's first settler was Captain Ebenezer Hovey from Charlotte, Vermont.

The arrival of railroads around midcentury sparked the area's development as a resort. The next peaceful invasion came with wealthy Americans investing in vacation homes. Among them was Henry Atkinson, president of the Georgia Electric Light Company, who in 1900 built the mansion that is now the inn. Hovey Manor is a replica of George Washington's home at Mount Vernon.

Yet as time passed, estates of this size became increasingly hard to maintain. In 1950, the inn entered its next phase of existence. The man who introduced and

PREVIOUS PAGES, Hovey Manor, viewed from the frozen lake in Quebec's Eastern Townships. Looking very much like Mount Vernon, George Washington's home, it is in fact a copy built by a Georgia millionaire.

RIGHT, the "contemporary" cuisine presided over by the Belgian chef Mark deCanck exhibits a strong continental influence.

inspired inn travel here was Robert Brown, who had trained in hotel management in the U.S. and worked for Canada's leading hotel chain. He bestowed the name honoring the town's first settler.

Although the early years were a struggle, the inn quickly earned an outstanding reputation as one of the finest establishments in the Townships. In recent years, this solid base has only been improved upon by its present owners, Stephen and Kathryn Stafford. More gracious hosts cannot be found.

Although the inn has been expanded and modernized—particularly the bedrooms, where baths and a few jacuzzis have been added—the spirit of its elegant past has been preserved. Many of the rooms have fireplaces and a few have balconies.

The dining room has a new extension where at night the lights wink back from across the lake, but in the original part, the Colonial style fireplace is the main attraction. Antiques "Canadiana" are everywhere.

The Tap Room, a converted stable, is characterized by strictly French antecedents in the fixtures as well as the barnwood and log rafters retained for the interior. One section has a fireplace and high ceilings with a very rare Naskapi Indian canoe suspended overhead. Another section has a lower ceiling and enclosed booths which lend the more intimate feeling of an old tavern. An enclosed, second-story walkway connects this room with the main building. Cottages farther along the lakefront offer more individual privacy.

Belgian chef Mark de Canck's cuisine, which Steve labels "contemporary," rates an extended stay just to explore its variety. With an excellent wine cellar to boot, the inn earns one of the highest ratings given by the provincial hotel guide.

HOVEY MANOR SKIING

Hovey Manor has added cross country skiing to its year-round outdoor offerings through a cooperative effort with other resorts in the Lake Massawippi region. The inn offers thirty-five kilometers of groomed trails, twenty-five kilometers considered intermediate level and the remainder, beginner. Between the manor and the village are a number of trails that interconnect on the low hills that run along the western side of the lake.

There is something to test all abilities here. Beginners may find it easiest to practice on the frozen lake surface. Hardier types can make extended trips on the long trail to the lower end of the lake, passing through nearby farmland and over wooded bluffs. A favorite destination is a children's camp near Katevale about ten kilometers away, which has a public cafeteria. The site, high above the lake, has a spectacular panorama.

The Manor cooperates with two other resorts on Massawippi for an inn-to-inn midweek stay that takes skiers on a 25-kilometer tour of its entire length. Included in the package are day trips to other ski touring centers such as Mt. Orford Provincial Park, the site of one of Canada's top alpine centers.

Guests frequently ski on the trails or across the lake to explore the village, which has boutiques and antique shops. The countryside east of the lake has rolling farmland, substantial homes, and villages reminiscent of New England. Free privileges are available at an indoor racquet club nearby, and Montreal is little more than an hour away.

RIGHT, solicitous service and a reputable wine cellar contribute to dining pleasure. The guest rooms combine period pieces with modern comfort.

L'AUBERGE DU VIEUX FOYER

A modern inn with a difference

LEFT, the chalet-style inn, with the provincial Quebec flag flying, fits snugly into the Lauretian landscape. Natural wood, leaded glass, and other innovative touches make for interesting interiors, as in the dining room, LEFT, and the bar, BELOW.

MICHEL GIROUX decided at 20 that he wanted to be an innkeeper. Then a student working at a hotel in Montreal, he'd been coming on holidays to a cottage he shared with two cousins in Val David. When a small inn there was put up for sale, Michel persuaded them to invest with him in his dream. Jocelyn, who had hotel school training in Switzerland and experience with two prestigious Canadian establish-

ments to his credit, quit his job to share the innkeeping duties.

The result is a marvelous cultural mix. They took an inn originally opened by an Italian, added two Canadians with Swiss backgrounds, hired a young French chef ready to test his skills (now a partner), and have assembled a modern inn with a difference.

Michel doesn't feel that his Swiss roots have any influence on his inclinations as an innkeeper. "I am thinking toward the future," he says with élan, "not like most Europeans, to the past." The inn decor confirms this in dozens of ways that delight the eye or enhance the comfort. He calls it "our style . . . not art deco, not modern, not old." Pleasing, it definitely is.

The chalet-style building, which is only about thirty years old, retains its European atmosphere despite several expansions. The "old fireplace" that gives the inn its name remains the focal point of the common room. Converting the entrance to the adjacent dining room to a diagonal wall was a masterful stroke that changes the perspective and transforms one corner into a quiet conversation nook.

There are two dining rooms. The original one is small and warmed by knotty pine walls, handcrafted wooden tables and numerous plants. An addition at the rear of the inn overlooking a small lake has clean, modern lines and an airy aspect created by two walls of windows and skylights. The bar is tucked into one corner of the room, and on the other side of the kitchen is a room suitable either for dining or meetings.

Another sign of its up-to-the-minute operation is the inn's "animateur," or

recreation director, who serves as a catalyst for entertainment during the week. Guests can be private if they choose or they can be part of the group for activities like nutty, "mix'em-up" games, fondue or casino parties, and sleighrides.

The cuisine is French and offers three or four table d'hôte meals plus à la carte choices. Outside diners are taken by reservation, and on the weekends there are two sittings. The exposure to a new cuisine and atmosphere is part of the attraction for Americans of a visit to the Laurentians, Michel feels. He adds, conversely, that getting to know Americans is also good for Canadians.

The inn's logo captures its spirit as well as any description. It depicts in silhouette the village's three mountains, popular with rock climbers, a stylized sun, and a spruce tree. Vigor, energy, and enthusiasm are the hallmarks here.

AUBERGE DU VIEUX FOYER SKIING

Val David has the atmosphere of a European resort town. People wander through the streets with their skis, propping them outside stores while making their purchases, and gathering at the coffee shops in the afternoon (or any time, for that matter) for energy replacement.

Thus the village becomes the principal target for guests starting out from Auberge du Vieux Foyer. They begin on a gradually expanding network of trails that surround the village and its several mountains. In other seasons, the trails are used for hiking and horseback riding.

The trail from the inn passes through neighbors' yards and then into conifers that line a small stream which flows along the base of Mont Plante and Mont Cesaire. In the beginning, the terrain seems the sort ideal for rabbit hunting and dippy bumps, but it leads to smoother sailing beyond. This is gentle skiing, for the most part, with frequent nice vistas of the nearby peaks.

For more serious skiers, there is a trail to the top of one of the mountains and a long-distance wilderness trek for hardy skiers only called the Gilespie. Beginners can ski along the railroad track that runs through town and follows in part the Rivière du Nord, passing several small lakes. There also is a camping area called Belle Etoile that gives its name to the trail past the inn. This moderate terrain is pleasing for those who want to get out and enjoy the countryside and woods without too strenuous a workout.

The inn, like the village where it is located, is strongly reminiscent of the European resort scene. The cuisine, of course, is French.

OTTER LAKE HAUS

An infectious zest for living

THE QUEBECOIS' zest for enjoying their leisure is infectious. Sitting in the dining room at the Otter Lake Haus, one quickly feels a part of the bubbling conversation, the frequent laughter, and the occasional verbal ex-

change across tables about the day's adventures.

The gaiety reflects, too, the congenial atmosphere that the Thiel family fosters. Fred and Aga came to the inn as guests when it was operated by its original owners, a German couple who established it in the thirties. When it became available for sale in 1970, the Thiels sold their Montreal business and moved their family to the country.

Since they were newcomers to the inn business, the first years were difficult, says Aga, but they've never regretted their decision. Their son Rick, after taking hotel training in Montreal and Europe followed by several years with a large chain in Canada, has joined the business.

Although leading Laurentian alpine centers are only a half-hour away, Otter Lake, Lac à la Loutre, seems a world apart. On the approach from the autoroute at St. Jovite, a huge massif soon appears

The inn is a haven surrounded by a range of skiing choices. Beginning at the back door, LEFT, one can explore the wooded mountainsides or play on the frozen surface of the lake in front of the inn RIGHT. As can be seen from the signs, it is useful to speak French, but not necessary.

to the west. After skirting the broad Ri-vière Rouge plain, the road at Huberdeau winds back into mountains from the south. The inn is located on the far side of the lake, which lies in the cone of an ancient volcano, 190 feet deep and circled by low peaks. The land beyond the inn on the lakeshore lies untouched, adding to the feeling of remoteness.

The inn itself is a sanctuary. A small, cozy living room with plenty of easy chairs and couches is brightened by a sunporch where the tables are busy with board and card games. In the combination bar and lounge area at the center of the house, wrought iron chandeliers crafted in Germany and old sporting equipment make good conversation pieces. Rick pre-sides here at the hub of activities, provid-ing advice about ski conditions and mis-cellaneous assistance.

Sitting rooms in the annex and "little house" near the lake offer alternative spaces, as does a tiny, second-floor porch in the main building which overlooks the lake. Some of the bedrooms are rustic, while others have peaked roofs and

Much of the food served at the inn is grown by the Thiel family, whose cuisine features both French and German dishes. RIGHT and BELOW, the beauty of winter and the solitude of a northern Laurentian retreat are readily ap-parent.

charming period furniture. The rooms in the main inn are named for German cities.

Outdoor recreation may be the excuse, but most guests come just to be at the inn and to enjoy its good food. Aga reigns in the kitchen, assisted by her husband and son at breakfast and additional staff at other meals. Both French and German dishes are specialities of the house. Three entrées are offered each evening plus soup, vegetable, salad bar, and Aga's special dessert concoctions. The Thiels grow a good deal of what reaches the tables in their nearby farm and gardens. They purchase only beef and fish.

OTTER LAKE HAUS SKIING

The Thiels have developed fifty kilometers of groomed and tracked trails with the cooperation of 26 private landowners who grant rights of way. The town Optimist Club helps maintain the trails as part of their activities for local youth, and they ask for a small contribution from those using the trails.

Many guests prefer skiing on the lake or the nearly level shore trail. There is an easy route through the woods to the village for shopping or lunch. An abandoned railroad track appeals to average skiers, although this has been designated also as snowmobile territory.

One popular but more difficult trail climbs through a beautiful, wide ravine behind the inn, circles the far side of the mountain west of the lake and returns via the lakeshore trails. A long downhill run about three-quarters of the way is its special attraction. Rugged rock formations and wide vistas add interest as well. Trails branch off from this one to the top of the mountain and to longer trips beyond it. These are recommended for experienced skiers who can handle more difficult terrain. Guide service can be arranged.

The countryside, with its many lakes and old houses built in the characteristic French-Canadian style of log and stone, is worth touring by car. The village is the site of religious pilgrimages to the Calvaire d'Huberdeau, huge stone statues depicting the stations of the cross brought from Belgium and erected at a former monastery.

FAR HILLS INN

Comfort with a cosmopolitan twist

FAR HILLS INN has hosted NATO conferees, international Olympic delegates, members of Parliament, and famous artists and writers. But what is important to its guests is that they have found a place with superb service, an outstanding cuisine and an ambience rare on any continent. This is comfort with a cosmopolitan twist.

The tone is perhaps a bit more brisk in winter, when most guests come especially for cross country skiing. Even those who arrive late in the day are eager to get away to the trails for a quick outing soon after they have checked in.

There is a blend of accessible outdoor recreation in any season and leisurely recovery in distinctively decorated rooms. The tempo, definitely upbeat, is variable, determined by the cast of characters drawn here at any one time and the correlating elements of the inn itself. Handpainted murals of characteristic Quebec scenes make a conversation piece of the fireplace in the capacious and inviting main com-

TOP LEFT, even average skiers can attain this view of the undulating Laurentian landscape from the top of Iceberg Mountain. BOTTOM, the starting point for touring the varied trails of the region. RIGHT, ski instructor Ernest de Alcala. BELOW, innkeepers David and Louise Pemberton-Smith have made this one of Canada's premier resorts, a view of which is shown OVERLEAF.

mon room. The murals, done by a Swiss painter who lived nearby, decorate many unexpected places, including stairways and guestrooms.

In the cocktail lounge, the windows that overlook the "far hills" (hence the "Far Hills" Inn) are the main attraction. Favored for quick lunches during the day, this area becomes a piano bar at night.

Windows on three sides make the dining room cheerful in daylight and enhance the candlelight at night. The inn cuisine is continental with a French-Canadian influence and is supervised by chef Jacques-Louis Brunelle, whose career has taken him from Switzerland to the Bahamas before coming to Canada. The choices are mind-boggling and the ultimate effect, sheer pleasure.

Far Hills is a unique experience. The combination of modern facilities (the inn is not yet fifty years old), setting, and

atmosphere sets standards enviable among North American resorts. The aim of innkeepers David and Louise Pemberton Smith is constant improvement. For instance, they recently added an indoor squash court.

They have brought the inn a long way from its situation in the late sixties, when it was owned by a holding company in Montreal that hired David to rescue it among several failing operations. In 1970, he asked Louise to take over the inn, and five years later they not only had revived it but decided it was worth their own investment. Their personal involvement makes the difference.

Louise, formerly a nurse, finds that caring for people is similar in the inn business. She has imparted to her staff her philosophy of giving undiluted attention to guests' needs. David supplies a fine eye for detail and business that supports her flair and enthusiasm. Together they make a great team.

FAR HILLS INN SKIING

David Pemberton Smith has developed what is beyond doubt the largest and probably the oldest cross country skiing center in eastern Canada. There are 125 kilometers of trails in the vicinity of the inn.

Indoor facilities include cuisine and service, ABOVE, that sets levels of excellence difficult to duplicate anywhere else in North America. The guest rooms, LEFT, are restful retreats done in a variety of styles, and the pool, BELOW, is part of the recreation center.

RIGHT, the inn setting provides unparalleled opportunities for enjoying the out-of-doors in all seasons, but particularly in winter.

Not many ski areas of any size, anywhere, can claim a mountain that average skiers can handle with ease. The one rising behind the inn, called Iceberg, is completely at odds with its name and the inn's welcoming spirit. Two overlooks provide a 360-degree view of the countryside, composed on all sides by small lakes surrounded by low mountains. The trail back to the inn crosses Lake Lavallee, where guests enjoy water sports (sans motors) in warm weather.

The Far Hills Touring Center network has incredible variation is terrain, but average skiers have no trouble with most trails. There are equally inspiring vistas from many vantage points. The touring center staff conducts guided tours regularly so that inexperienced skiers may try more demanding trails. In the course of a midweek stay, most skiers will have a chance to become familiar with the entire network.

There are challenging passages for advanced skiers as well, including trails to other nearby peaks. The center also links with several wilderness trails, and the Maple Leaf, originally intended to cross the entire Laurentian region, traverses the inn system as well.

Well-known alpine centers are within easy driving range, but most inn guests are drawn to its cross country trails.

THE INN ON THE COMMON. Main Street, Craftsbury Common, VT 05827; (802) 586-9619; Penny and Michael Schmitt, Innkeepers. Open all year. **Rates:** Moderate to expensive; includes full breakfast and dinner. **Accommodations:** 18 rooms, 14 with private baths, 4 sharing. Dining room serves breakfast and dinner to guests only. Liquor served. Children accepted; pets accepted, with notice; smoking allowed; Visa, MasterCard, personal checks accepted. **Winter facilities:** (at ski center) sauna; nautilus equipment; ice skating (sometimes); tobogganing; ski equipment rental and sales; ski instruction; guide service; lunch and refreshments; warming huts.

Directions: from South, take I-91 to St. Johnsbury exit and Rte. 2 west to Rte. 15. Go west on 15 to Hardwick and take Rte. 14 north 8 miles to turnoff on right for Craftsbury; 3 miles to village and inn. Will pick up Burlington, Montpelier, and Stowe/Morrisville for train, bus, or plane.

EDSON HILL MANOR, Edson Hill Road, Box 2480, RR 1, Stowe, VT 05672; (802) 253-7371; Laurence P. Heath, Jr. and Anita B. Heath, co-Innkeepers. Open all year. **Rates:** moderate; includes breakfast and dinner. **Accommodations:** 26 rooms, 11 in manor and 15 in carriage houses, 20 with fireplaces, 22 with private baths, 4 sharing. Restaurant serves meals to guests and public. Liquor served. Children accepted (under 12, $36 ea.); no pets; Visa MasterCard, American Express accepted. **Winter facilities:** sleighrides; tobogganing; winter horseback riding. **Ski shop:** equipment rental; ski instruction; guide service; refreshments; warming huts; special services include waxing and repairs.

Directions: from Burlington take I-89 south to exit 10. Go north on Rte. 100 ten miles to Rte. 108 north for 3.1 miles and turn right on Edson Hill Road for 2 miles. There is a shuttlebus from Burlington to Stowe for those who take bus, Amtrak, or plane there.

TUCKER HILL LODGE, RD 1, Box 147 (Route 17), Waitsfield, VT 05673; (802) 496-3983; Zeke and Emily Church, Innkeepers. Open all year for lodging, dinner in season. **Rates:** inexpensive to moderate; includes breakfast and dinner. **Accommodations:** 20 rooms, 14 with private baths, 6 sharing. Restaurant open to guests and public, with taped classical music at breakfast and light jazz at dinner. Liquor served. Children accepted at same rates as adults; no pets; smoking allowed; Visa, MasterCard, American Express, Diners accepted. Some French spoken. **Ski Shop:** equipment rental and sales, including some clothes; ski instruction includes telemark; light lunch of soup/chili and refreshments served; special services include an elementary school program and video tape for lessons.

Directions: from Burlington south on I-89 take exit 10 at Waterbury. Go south on Rte. 100 for 12 miles, then west on Rte. 17 for 1½ miles to the inn. From Montpelier, go north on I-89 to exit 9, follow Rte. 100B to Rte. 100 to Rte. 17 to inn. Pickups arranged at Waterbury, Montpelier, and Burlington airport.

MOUNTAIN TOP CROSS COUNTRY SKI RESORT, Mountain Top Road, Chittenden, VT 05737; (800) 445-2100, (802) 483-2311; William P. Wolfe, Mgr. Open all year. **Rates:** moderate; includes breakfast and dinner. **Accommodations:** 35 rooms, all with private baths; 15 cottages. Dining room serves 3 meals daily to guests and public. Liquor served. Children allowed; no pets; smoking allowed; Visa, MasterCard, American Express accepted. **Winter facilities:** sauna; Jacuzzi; ice skating; ping pong; tobogganing, sleigh rides. **Ski shop:** equipment rental, including skis and snowshoes; equipment and clothing sales; ski instruction; guide service; lunch; warming huts; first aid.

Directions: from Rutland, Vermont, take Rte. 7 north to Chittenden Road (at country store); go north through Chittenden to inn situated north of Chittenden overlooking the reservoir.

WOODSTOCK INN AND RESORT, 14 The Green, Woodstock, VT 05091; (802) 457-1100; Lee Bowden, Manager. Open all year. **Rates:** Moderate to expensive, no meals included. **Accommodations:** 120 rooms, 2 townhouses, 1 guest house, all with private baths. Coffee shop, main dining room and lounge serve breakfast, lunch and dinner to guests and public. Liquor served at the inn, touring center, and sports center. English, German, Spanish, French spoken; major credit cards accepted. Entertainment Fridays and Saturdays in lounge, nightly in main dining room. **Winter facilities:** new sports center housing swimming; sauna; Jacuzzi; hot tub; nautilus; racquetball; squash; indoor tennis; ping pong; nearby ice skating. **Ski shop:** equipment rental; clothes and equipment sales; ski instructions, all levels; guide service; lunch, bar, refreshments; warming huts at sports center; health center nearby, first aid.

Directions: located on the common at Woodstock, Vermont. From junction of I-91 and I-89 in White River Junction go north on I-89. Take exit 1 to Woodstock which is 12 miles west on Route 4 to the Village Green and the Woodstock Inn.

THE VILLAGE INN AT LANDGROVE, RFD Box 215, Landgrove, VT 05148; (802) 824-6673; Jay and Kathy Snyder, Innkeepers. Open December 15 to April 1 and June 15 to October 15. **Rates:** inexpensive to moderate; includes full breakfast and dinner. **Accommodations:** 14 rooms with private baths, 6 rooms with shared baths. Restaurant serves guests and public. Liquor served. Children welcome; no pets; no smoking; Visa, MasterCard, American Express accepted. **Winter facilities:** hot tub, paddle tennis, sleigh rides. **Ski shop:** Guide service, lunch on request for guests only.

Directions: from I-92 take exit 6 onto Rte. 103 to Chester, then Rte. 11 to Londonderry. About ½ mile past shopping center turn right on Landgrove Road to village. After crossing bridge, bear left for 1 mile to inn.

The rates at the inns are evaluated as follows (*per person double occupancy, including breakfast and dinner*)

Inexpensive: under $55 • Moderate: $55 to $75 • Expensive: over $75

WINDHAM HILL INN, RR 1, Box 44, West Townshend, VT 05359; (802) 874-4080; Ken and Linda Busteed, Owner/Innkeepers. Open all year except April and November. **Rates:** moderate. **Accommodations:** 10 rooms in main house and 5 rooms in recently renovated barn, all with private baths. Full service dining room for inn guests only, no lunch. Liquor served. Children 12 years and older welcome (adult rates apply); no pets; Visa, MasterCard accepted. **Winter facilities:** ice skating. **Ski shop:** equipment rental; ski instruction; guide service; warming huts; first aid.

Directions: from Boston take Mass Rte. 2 to Greenfield MA and I-91 north. Take I-91 to VT exit 2, VT Rte. 9 east to Brattleboro, VT and VT Rte. 30 north. Go 22 miles to the turn off to the inn. Take a right turn onto the road to Windham for 1½ miles to inn entrance.

THE HERMITAGE INN, Coldbrook Road, Wilmington, VT 05363; (802) 464-3511; James L. McGovern, Innkeeper. Open all year. **Rates:** moderate to expensive; includes full breakfast and dinner. **Accommodations:** 29 rooms, 25 with private baths, 4 sharing. Restaurant serves dinner nightly, soup and sandwich daily in winter, brunch on holidays and weekends to guests and public. Liquor served. Children welcome (same rates apply); no pets; French and German spoken; major credit cards accepted in dining room. **Ski shop:** equipment rental; sales of clothes and some equipment; ski instruction; guide service; lunch and snacks; toboggan and snow shoe rental; telemark rental and lessons; Ridge Trail tours; first aid.

Directions: from Wilmington go 2½ miles on Rte. 100 north and turn left onto Coldbrook Road. Go 3 miles and Hermitage is on the left. Private plane pickup from Mt. Snow Airport available.

THE INN AT THORN HILL, Thorn Hill Road, Jackson, NH 03846; (603) 383-4242; Bob and Pattie Guindon, Innkeepers. Open all year. **Rates:** moderate; includes full breakfast and gourmet dinner. **Accommodations:** 9 rooms, 3 cottages, 7 rooms in carriage house, all with private baths. Restaurant holds 44 per seating, 2 seatings per evening; dinner 6–9 P.M. by reservation. Liquor served. Children over six welcome; no pets; smoking allowed; Visa, MasterCard, American Express accepted. **Winter facilities:** swimming; sauna; Jacuzzi; nautilus; raquetball; indoor tennis nearby. Ice skating; tobogganing; heated wax room; sleigh rides.

Directions: information supplied on reservation.

THE BALSAMS Grand Resort Hotel and Wilderness Downhill and Cross Country Ski Area, Route 26, Dixville Notch, NH 03576; (603) 255-3400, in continental U.S. (800) 255-0600, in NH (800) 255-0800; Warren Pearson and Stephen Barba, Innkeepers. Open all year except mid-Oct. to mid-Dec. and April 1 to mid-May. **Rates:** moderate to expensive: includes breakfast and dinner. **Accommodations:** 232 rooms with private baths. Dining room serves breakfast and dinner to guests and public. Liquor served in 4 lounges; folk singers, pianists, top 40 bands, cabaret acts. Children welcome ($25/night minimum or $5 × age of child up to the adult rate); no pets; designated non-smoking area in dining room; French spoken; Visa, MasterCard, American Express accepted. **Winter facilities:** ping pong; ice skating; tobogganing; wilderness downhill ski area (12 downhill trails, 3 lifts, 1,000 foot vertical drop). **Ski shop:** equipment rental; full service ski shop; ski instruction; a la carte lunch; nursery; special tours; full service video and recreation department; medical services; first aid.

Directions: from Boston: go north to the end of I-93 at Franconia Notch, NH then take Rte. 3 to Colebrook, NH and go east on Rte. 26 to Dixville Notch. Alternate Rte. from Boston; Rte. 95 to Portsmouth, then Rte. 16 to Rte. 26, then west on Rte. 26 to Dixville Notch, or Rte. 95 from Boston to Maine Tpke., leave at Exit 11, then Rte. 26 to Dixville Notch.

THE NOTCHLAND INN, Hart's Location, NH 03812; (603) 374-6131; Pat and John Bernardin, Innkeepers. Open all year. **Rates:** moderate. **Accommodations:** 10 rooms, 4 rooms in guesthouses, all private baths and working fireplaces. Dining room serves dinner to guests and public. BYOB allowed. Children at half adult rate; no pets; designated smoking areas; Visa, MasterCard, American Express. **Winter facilities:** sauna; hot tub; ice skating; sledding. **Ski shop:** equipment rental by arrangement; ski instruction; guide service; lunch by arrangement; refreshments; medical services; first aid.

Directions: from Boston take I-95 north to Rte. 16 north toward North Conway to Rte. 302 north about 20 minutes into the White Mountains National Forest. Alternate route from Boston take Rte. 93 north to Rte. 3 north to Twin Mountain then go south on Rte. 302 15 minutes to White Mountain National Forest. Pickups available.

THE NEW ENGLAND INN, Route 16A at the Intervale, North Conway, NH 03860; (603) 356-5541; Linda and Joe Johnston, Innkeepers. Open all year except April and first 2 weeks in May. **Rates:** moderate to expensive; includes breakfast and dinner. **Accommodations:** 12 rooms, 10 cottages, 4 single village house suites, 12 rooms in annexes, all private baths. Restaurant serves dinner to guests and public. Liquor served. Live entertainment. Children welcome (takes additional person rate); no pets; smoking allowed; Visa, MasterCard, American Express accepted. **Ski shop:** equipment rental; equipment sales; ski instruction; guide service; refreshments; medical services; first aid.

Directions: from Portland take Rte. 302 west to Rte. 16 to Intervale. From Boston take I-95 north to Spaulding Tpke. to Rte. 16 to Intervale. Pickups available.

SNOWVILLAGE INN, Snowville, NH 03849; (603) 447-2818; Ginger Blymyer, Owner. Open all year except April and May. **Rates:** Moderate to expensive; includes full breakfast and dinner. **Accommodations:** 15 rooms, all with private baths. Restaurant serves dinner to guests and public; seats 45–50. Liquor served. Children welcome ($15–30 per day depending on age); pets allowed; smoking allowed except in main dining room; French, some Spanish spoken; Visa, MasterCard, American Express accepted. **Winter facilities:** sauna; ice skating; sledding; tobogganing. **Ski shop:** equipment rental; ski instruction; packed lunch; refreshments.

Directions: from Boston take I-95 north to Spaulding Tpke. to Rte. 16 north. to Conway then take Rte. 153 south 5 miles to Crystal Lake. Turn left into Snowville and follow signs to the Inn. Pickups available from Conway area.

MOOSE MOUNTAIN LODGE, Etna, NH 03750; (603) 643-3529; Kay and Peter Shumway, Owner/Innkeepers. Open December 26 to March 31 and June 1 to November 1. **Rates:** includes full breakfast and dinner. **Accommodations:** 12 rooms, 5 shared baths. Restaurant serves guests only. BYOB. Children welcome five and older; no pets; smoking limited; some French and Spanish; Visa and MasterCard accepted. **Winter facilities:** ping pong; player piano; ice skating. **Ski shop:** equipment rental; guide service; lunch and refreshments for guests; pick-up service at end of long trails.

Directions: from exit 18 on Rte. 89 go north on Rte. 120 toward Hanover for ½ mile. Turn right on Etna Road; ½ mile past Etna Store turn right onto Rudsboro Road. Follow it for two miles then turn left onto Dana Road for ½ mile. Turn right on road to lodge.

FOLLANSBEE INN, P.O. Box 92, North Sutton, NH 03260; (603) 927-4221; Dick and Sandy Reilein, Innkeepers. Open all year except parts of November and April. **Rates:** Moderate; includes full country breakfast. **Accommodations:** 23 rooms, 11 with private baths, 12 sharing. Restaurant serves dinner to guests and public, breakfast to guests only. Liquor served. Children welcome over eight (third person in room $15–$20); no pets; completely non-smoking; Visa and MasterCard accepted. **Winter facilities:** ice skating; tobogganing. **Ski shop:** (at Norsk) equipment rental; sales of equipment and clothes; ski instruction; guide service; lunch; refreshments; warming huts.

Directions: two hours north of Boston take I-93 to Concord, NH then take I-89 to exit 10. Follow Blue Service signs to North Sutton. The Inn is behind a white church.

HIGHWINDS INN, Gore Mountain Road, North Creek, NY 12853; (518) 251-3435 weekdays, 251-3760 evenings and weekends; Kim Repscha, Innkeeper. Open all year. **Rates:** moderate; includes full breakfast and dinner. **Accommodations:** 4 rooms, 1 with private bath. Restaurant serves dinner to guests and public, reservations required. BYOB allowed. No pets; no credit cards. **Winter facilities:** pool table; snow shoeing; ice skating; tobogganing. **Ski shop:** guided cross country trips with lunch.

Directions: from Albany go north on Rte. 87 to exit 23, Warrensburg, then north on Rte. 9 to Rte. 28. Go north on Rte. 28 to North River, then left on Gore Mountain Road to High Winds. From Montreal and Buffalo take Rte. 8 to Rte. 28 north then go north on Rte. 28 to North River. Take a left on Gore Mountain Road to High Winds. Pick ups at train and bus stations available.

THE BARK EATER, Alstead Mill Road, Keene, NY 12942; (518) 576-2221; Joe Pete Wilson and Harley McDevitt Wilson, Innkeepers. Open all year. **Rates:** inexpensive; includes full breakfast. **Accommodations:** 16 rooms, 4 private baths, 4 shared. Dining room serves gourmet trail lunch and dinner to guests, public by reservation. Children allowed; limited policy on pets; designated smoking room; no credit cards. **Winter facilities** (nearby): swimming; indoor tennis; ice skating; curling; tobogganing. **Ski shop:** equipment rental and sales; ski instruction; guide service; lunch; warming huts; medical service; first aid.

Directions: from Albany take Rte. 87 north to exit 30, then take Rte. 73 west to one mile west of Keene. Take a right on Alstead Mill Road to inn.

GARNET HILL LODGE, 13th Lake Road, North River, NY 12856; (518) 251-2821; George and Mary Heim, Innkeepers. Open all year except for 2 weeks at Thanksgiving and 2 weeks in June. **Rates:** inexpensive; includes full breakfast and dinner. **Accommodations:** 26 rooms, 21 with private baths, 5 sharing. Restaurant serves 3 meals daily to guests and public; lunch 12–2 P.M., dinner 6–9 P.M. Liquor served. Children welcome; no pets; no credit cards, personal checks accepted. **Winter facilities:**

---

ice skating, tobogganing; game room. **Ski shop:** equipment rental and sales; ski instruction; guide service; refreshments; free bus pickup at far end of trail system; ski demonstrations; video movies and ski movies of guests and lecturers.

Directions: from Albany take I-87 north to exit 23 and go north on Rte. 9 to Rte. 28. Go north on Rte. 28 for 22 miles to North River and turn left onto 13th Loake Road for 4½ miles to lodge. Will pick up at Warrensburg for Trailways or Greyhound bus.

MOHONK MOUNTAIN HOUSE, Mohonk Lake, New Paltz, NY 12561; (914) 255-1000; the Smiley Brothers, Innkeepers. Open all year. **Rates:** inexpensive, moderate, and expensive; includes breakfast, lunch, and dinner. **Accommodations:** 200 rooms, some with private baths, some sharing. Dining room serves 3 meals daily to guests and public. No bars or lounges; alcohol served with evening meal only; also available for consumption in guest rooms. Entertainment includes classical music concerts, dancing, slideshows, children's program, and movies. Children welcome at $30 each (12 and under) if sharing with 2 adults; no pets; Visa, MasterCard, American Express accepted. **Winter facilities:** sauna, Universal equipment for working out, platform tennis, ping pong, ice skating, snow tubing. **Ski shops:** equipment rentals; ski instruction; guide service; lunch and refreshments at day center lodge; first aid.

Directions: from New York State Thruway take exit 18 at New Paltz and turn left and follow Main Street through New Paltz to the bridge over the Wallkill River. Cross bridge and turn right at "Mohonk" sign. Bear left and follow Mountain Rest Road to inn.

THE INN AT STARLIGHT LAKE, Starlight, PA 18461; (717) 798-2519; Jack and Judy McMahon, Innkeepers. Open all year except last Sunday of March to April 16. **Rates:** inexpensive to moderate; includes full breakfast and dinner. **Accommodations:** 27 rooms, most with private baths; dorms. Restaurant serves lunch and dinner to guests and public. Liquor served. BYOB in rooms only. Live and canned entertainment. Children 5 and over allowed ($37 in same room with adults); no pets; smoking allowed; Visa, MasterCard accepted. **Winter facilities:** ping pong; ice skating; sledding. **Ski shop:** equipment rental; ski instruction; lunch; refreshments; medical services; first aid.

Directions: from I-81 take exit 62 to Rte. 107 east into Rte. 247 to Forest City. Turn left on Rte. 171.

SUNDAY RIVER INN, RFD 2, Box 1688, Bethel, ME 04217; (207) 824-2410; Steve and Peggy Wight, Innkeepers. Open November 15 to April 15. **Rates:** inexpensive; includes full breakfast and dinner. **Accommodations:** Dining room serves breakfast and dinner to guests only. BYOB allowed. Children allowed 12 and under (in room with adults $20); no pets; non-smoking atmosphere preferred; Visa, MasterCard accepted. **Winter facilities:** sauna; ice skating; ping pong; tobogganing. **Ski shop:** equipment rental; equipment and clothing sales; ski instruction; guide service; lunch; refreshments; warming hut at Base Lodge; first aid.

Directions: information from inn on reservation.

LITTLE LYFORD POND LODGE, Box 688, Brownville, ME 04404; (207) 695-2821; Joel Frantzman, Owner. Open all year. **Rates:** moderate; includes all meals. **Accommodations:** 6 cabins with outhouse and sauna. BYOB allowed. Children allowed (under 15 half price, family rates on request); pets allowed;